COME ON CHURCH!
WAKE UP!

Sin Within the Church and What Jesus Has To Say About It

MICHELE NEAL

CREATION
HOUSE

Come on Church! Wake Up! by Michele Neal
Published by Creation House
A Charisma Media Company
600 Rinehart Road
Lake Mary, Florida 32746
www.charismamedia.com

Unless otherwise indicated, all Scripture quotations are taken from the Holy Bible, New Living Translation, copyright © 1996, 2004, 2007 by Tyndale House Foundation. Used by permission of Tyndale House Publishers, Inc., Carol Stream, Illinois 60188. All rights reserved.

Scripture quotations marked KJV are from the King James Version of the Bible.

Scripture quotations marked NIV are from the Holy Bible, New International Version. Copyright © 1973, 1978, 1984, 2010, 2011, International Bible Society. Used by permission.

Scripture quotations marked NKJV are from the New King James Version of the Bible. Copyright © 1979, 1980, 1982 by Thomas Nelson, Inc., publishers. Used by permission.

Some Scripture quotations and commentary taken from the *Life Application Study Bible, New King James Version* (Carol Stream, IL: Tyndale House, 2000).

Design Director: Bill Johnson
Cover design by Terry Clifton

Visit the author's website: www.comeonchurchwakeup.com

Library of Congress Cataloging-in-Publication Data: 2012948814
International Standard Book Number: 978-1-62136-316-3
E-book International Standard Book Number: 978-1-62136-315-6

While the author has made every effort to provide accurate telephone numbers and Internet addresses at the time of publication, neither the publisher nor the author assumes any responsibility for errors or for changes that occur after publication.

First edition

12 13 14 15 16 — 9 8 7 6 5 4 3 2 1
Printed in Canada

DEDICATION

*I dedicate this book to my heavenly Father,
His Son Jesus Christ who is my Lord and
Savior, and to the Holy Spirit who lives and
dwells in me through my faith in Jesus Christ.*

*May the fruit that is born from the publishing
of this book bring glory and honor to the
Lord, for this is His work and His book.*

*I am simply His servant, the vessel He has
used to fulfill His purpose.*

ACKNOWLEDGMENTS

FIRSTLY, I GIVE thanks and glory to God for choosing and enabling me to write this book. I did not previously possess an adequate understanding of the message of this book. What I have written was revealed to me by the Lord at the beginning of a "strange affliction," which you will read about in chapter 1. The writing of this book came suddenly—like a bolt of lightning—in the most strange of circumstances, that I have no doubt in my mind of its divine origin. Thank You, Lord.

My thanks also go to my wonderful and longsuffering husband, Chris, for sharing with me in my sufferings throughout our six years together. You are an amazing man of God with the most teachable spirit that any wife could wish for. Thank you for accompanying me in this journey. I know that the Lord opened your eyes at the same time as He opened mine, but neither of us knew until I began to share with you what He was showing me. I remember how our mouths fell wide open in utter astonishment! Thank you, darling, for listening to me read the entire manuscript out loud and for painstakingly proofreading it and making the necessary corrections. Thank you for your patience toward my lack of technical ability. I am slowly acquainting myself with the requirements of the twenty-first century!

Thanks, also, to my beautiful daughter, Emma Crago, who joined in listening to me read the draft manuscript and who has also stood by me and comforted me through much fear and trembling and through many tears in the writing of this book. Emma, you are such a precious gift from God! I love you!

Also, I want to thank my twin sister, Sharon Cooper, for being there through the thick and thin of life on earth. God gave me a special gift when He decided to create us as twins! Thank you, sis, for your never-ending love to all of us. We love you very much!

I am also thankful to a young man, Steve Ellis, who rose to the challenge of typing the manuscript from my original handwritten pages. What an enormous undertaking that was! My computer skills are somewhat limited, and the prospect of doing the typing myself was an insurmountable obstacle. Thank you, Steve, for taking this burden off of me and for being a good and faithful servant of the Lord.

Finally, I would like to thank all the staff at Charisma Media/Creation House Publishers for accepting the manuscript and agreeing to publish the book, and with such an incredibly powerful cover design! Thank you SO much! The Lord led me to submit the manuscript to you and instructed me to leave it all in His hands. The book is now finished but the Lord's work has just begun. My part was to plant the seed; your part was to water it; God will produce the harvest for His glory! Amen!

This is a revelation from Jesus Christ, which God gave him to show his servants the events that must soon take place. He sent an angel to present this revelation to his servant John, who faithfully reported everything he saw. This is his report of the Word of God and the testimony of Jesus Christ. God blesses the one who reads the words of this prophecy to the church, and he blesses all who listen to its message and obey what it says, for the time is near.

—REVELATION 1:1–3

These are words of Jesus Christ to the churches from the Book of Revelation:

Anyone with ears to hear must listen to the Spirit and understand what He is saying to the churches.

—REVELATION 2:7, 11, 17; 3:6, 13, 22

Wake up! Strengthen what little remains, for even what is left is almost dead. *I find that your actions do not meet the requirements of my God.*

—REVELATION 3:2, EMPHASIS ADDED

Now go and write down these words. Write them in a book. They will stand until the end of time as a witness that these people are stubborn rebels who refuse to pay attention to the Lord's instructions. They tell the seers, "Stop seeing visions!" They tell the prophets, "Don't tell us what is right. Tell us nice things. Tell us lies. Forget all this gloom. Get off your narrow path."

—ISAIAH 30:8–11A

CONTENTS

PREFACE

THIS WORK IS of God. I know that because I know my wife. Michele is a servant of the living God but she has no theological qualifications. Like Peter, the disciple, she is an ordinary untrained person but she loves Jesus Christ. I have witnessed firsthand what it has taken for her to obey the Lord's call on her life to fulfill this work.

This book may appear controversial to many, but it is not. It is challenging. It could even cause an uproar. That's good, because that's what happened when Jesus spoke the hard truths that people resisted and rejected two thousand years ago. He challenged sin wherever He saw it.

This book is full of grace and hope too. So it should be—it's based entirely on Scripture, on both Jesus' warnings and His promises to His church.

You will have to decide for yourself. Is this an important, gracious, end-times warning from Almighty God to the church He loves, or is it simply the thoughts and views of a human being?

Whatever you decide, I personally believe that anyone who reads this book and ignores Jesus' warnings to His church does so at their peril.

I would implore you to read this book and find the courage to respond to what Jesus is saying. You will not regret it.

—CHRIS NEAL
SEPTEMBER 2012

Chapter 1

THE REASON FOR THIS BOOK

October 30, 2011

IN 1992 I became a born-again Christian, was baptized by full immersion, and was filled with the Holy Spirit as recorded on the Day of Pentecost in Acts 2:1–4. I am a housewife and the mother of a beautiful twenty-one-year-old daughter. I have spent all of my Christian life being a homemaker and raising my daughter, occasionally doing small jobs for people to earn a bit of pocket money.

When my daughter was born, I became very unwell with chronic fatigue syndrome and various associated symptoms that have caused me to really seek the Lord for His strength each day in order to be able to function. For many years I have not been able to attend church in the mornings because that is when the symptoms are worst. They improve by the afternoon, and now I am able to get to church for the evening services.

Over the past twenty years, the Lord has taken me through some very difficult times. As a result, I have spent a large amount of time alone in my "closet," reading the Word of God, praying, weeping, singing, and worshiping the Lord as the Holy Spirit has led me. The Lord has been my strength through everything, even through the pain and confusion of having to endure long-term health issues.

God has healed me of many things over the years, but the chronic fatigue and other symptoms in the mornings are an area of my life that for some reason I still have to bear. The fruit of this suffering is that it enables me to focus on the Lord and spend time with Him alone each day.

I have read the Book of Revelation on many occasions during the past twenty years. At first I wondered what it was all about, but gradually the Lord has been making things more clear to me as the years have gone by.

I have always been in awe of what awaits God's children when Jesus returns and we are called up to meet God in heaven. By "God's children" I mean those who, through their faith in Jesus Christ, have been "adopted" by God as His own children and have the right to be called children of God. The apostle John said of Jesus:

> He came into the very world He created, but the world didn't recognize Him. He came to His own people, and even they rejected Him. But to all who believed Him and accepted Him, He gave the right to become children of God.
>
> —JOHN 1:10–12

While I was seeking the Lord one day a few years ago, I felt God say to me the words: "Wake up, church!" The message hit me so powerfully that I decided to write it down so that I wouldn't forget it. I also felt very strongly that the Lord was asking me to write a book. Since I had never written a book before, I knew that I could not attempt to do this in my own strength. I knew that if God is commanding His church to "wake up," the message must be *very* important to Him and that He intends it to be for every Christian church on the face of the earth, for all time until Jesus returns.

Time went by, and although I felt God had given me the words, "Wake up, church," I didn't know what He wanted to wake the church up about, so I just carried on with my daily life as a believer and as a housewife and mother. Two years went by, and all the time, "Wake up, church," echoed in my mind.

In the summer of 2011, I was suddenly troubled with the smell of smoke. Although there was no smoke anywhere, I could smell it everywhere I went. Even when I drove three hours into a different county, the smell was still there. I had trouble getting to sleep because every inhalation was like breathing in great lungfuls of smoke. It was very distressing. I asked other people if they could smell it, but no one could. I think they thought I was imagining things!

This plagued me all day, every day for a week. I did manage to get to sleep by using fragrant oil on a tissue that I held to my nose until I fell asleep. But the moment I woke up, the smoke smell was there, relentlessly tormenting me nonstop.

I considered seeing my doctor about it, but at that point I felt the Holy Spirit tell me to pray because it was a spiritual attack and that I was smelling the smoke of hell. I immediately prayed to the Lord, and I bound and cast out this demonic attack in Jesus' name. The smell of smoke instantly disappeared. Praise be to God! I was so thankful to the Lord for revealing this to me so that I could take hold of the authority that He has given me in Christ (and to every believer) to come against the works of darkness and cast them out in Jesus' name.

However, I did wonder why I had been subjected to such an attack. It seemed to be an isolated incident without any explanation. With no clarification as to what this was about, I again went back to my usual routine of being a housewife and mother.

A few months later in October 2011, two days before starting the writing of this book, I was suddenly afflicted with a strange illness which literally appeared out of nowhere in a matter of seconds. I was confined to my bed for two days in great distress and immense physical pain. I was continually restless and agitated, desperately seeking relief from all that I was experiencing. I could not understand what caused me to suddenly become so unwell.

Even though I had been a born-again Christian since 1992, this sudden affliction made me feel unsure of my eternal destiny. All of the sins that I had fallen into as a believer came crashing into my mind. The voice of Satan began tormenting my mind and mocking me, saying, "OK, so God has forgiven the sins you committed *before* you put your faith in Jesus; but you have committed detestable sins *since* you became a Christian. How could you possibly think that God can forgive you of these when you have trampled the blood of the Son of God underfoot and spat in the face of His sacrifice? What you have done deserves eternal punishment in hell!"

This was all I could hear, constantly. I was distraught beyond description. I could hardly eat or drink anything, and sweat poured out of my body in the utter agony that I was going through. I cried out to God for help.

As a believer, many times I had confessed these sins that I committed and asked God to forgive me. I felt that I had been genuine in my confession, often with many tears. Yet at times throughout my twenty years as a believer, I have struggled with thoughts and motives that would have the potential to lead me down the same sinful path. Despite all my previous confessing and pleading, I could not get totally free from these thoughts and motives. They would lurk up on me unexpectedly and attempt to trip me up again. I could not understand why this kept happening. It felt as if something was missing in my search for freedom from this relentless tyranny.

During the initial two days of this sudden affliction, I felt as if my whole mind, heart, soul, body, and spirit were engulfed in a raging battle. I felt as if I were perched on the edge of the pit of hell, looking down into the raging inferno of eternal tormenting flames and feeling the over-whelming agony of the indescribable and endless heat.

It is at this point that my mind was drawn back to the incident a couple of months before when I could smell the smoke of hell. And it seemed that God had been pre-paring me for what He was now showing me. Despite the immense physical and emotional distress I was experi-encing, I called out to the Lord to help me and show me what was happening and why, and what *He* wanted *me* to do. I began to realize this was more than just an illness.

I was due to start reading the Book of Revelation again in my daily readings. So despite feeling absolutely dreadful, with my whole body aching from head to foot and unable to get comfortable no matter what position I tried to lay in my bed, I began reading the Book of the Revelation of Jesus Christ once again.

I was immediately struck with knowledge and under-standing that the words contained in this book are not only Jesus' words to the churches at the time that the Revelation was given to the apostle John. They are Jesus' words to every single church on earth until Jesus returns to usher in the end of the world as we know it.

I feel that the title of this book, *Come on Church! Wake Up!* has the almighty power of God behind it. The words of this title have power, like God is a grabbing hold of His church (rather like a father grabbing hold of his rebellious child) and saying, "For goodness sake, will you wake up and listen to Me and do what I am commanding you to do, because the end is coming! If you don't wake up out of your indifference and complacency, there are spiritual consequences involved regardless of what theology you have studied and believed or what watered down version of the gospel you have heard and been deceived by. My Word alone is the truth; it is not to be interpreted, it is to be believed. Wake up! Believe it! Obey it!" That is the picture I get in my mind just from the title alone.

As I read the messages of Jesus Christ to the churches in chapters 2 and 3 of the Book of Revelation, I was overwhelmed by the Holy Spirit as the words I was reading became filled with power and life. In the Gospel of John 6:63, Jesus says to His disciples, "And the very words I have spoken to you are spirit and life."

After reading Jesus' messages to the churches, I was overtaken by a response in me that I had never experienced in twenty years of being a born-again, Spirit-filled believer. I can only describe it as the God-ordained, agonizing, and crushing experience of godly sorrow. This was beyond tears of regret or merely being sorry for my sins. It is a whole body experience that felt as if it would never end—until the Savior reached me with His powerful Word of truth. This called for my response of repentance and obedience.

Once this experience has occurred in your life, there is no alternative. The experience of real godly sorrow for the sins we commit as believers is not a five-minute weep. I experienced two days of "looking into the pit of hell," followed by several days of Jesus speaking to me from the

Book of Revelation about my sins as a believer. This He accompanied with His "gift" to me of unrelenting godly sorrow—rivers of tears that seemed endless and unstoppable. Relief and comfort were unobtainable until the work the Lord was doing in me had been completed.

This godly sorrow forced me to face the horrendous, ugly reality that I was capable of being deceived (by Satan) into thinking that I could sin as a believer and believe there would not be any spiritual consequences. Jesus was showing me the truth about this deception from His Word in the Book of Revelation.

I read a devotional by Oswald Chambers. There are a few entries that describe my experience perfectly. Below are excerpts from *My Utmost for His Highest*.

HAVE YOU FELT THE PAIN INFLICTED BY THE LORD?

Have you ever felt the pain, inflicted by the Lord, at the very centre of your being, deep down in the most sensitive area of your life? The devil never inflicts pain there, and neither can sin nor human emotions. Nothing can cut through to that part of our being but the Word of God.[1]

REPENTANCE

Godly sorrow produces repentance leading to salvation.
—2 CORINTHIANS 7:10

Conviction of sin is best described in the words:
My sins, my sins, my Savior,

How sad on Thee they fall.

Conviction of sin is one of the most uncommon things that ever happens to a person. It is the beginning of an understanding of God. Jesus Christ said that when the Holy Spirit came He would convict people of sin (see John 16:8). And when the Holy Spirit stirs a person's conscience and brings him into the presence of God, it is not that person's relationship with others that bothers him but his relationship with God—"Against You, You only, have I sinned, and done this evil in your sight..." (Psalm 51:4). The wonders of conviction of sin, forgiveness, and holiness are so interwoven that it is only the forgiven person who is truly holy. He proves he is forgiven by being the opposite of what he was previously, by the grace of God. Repentance always brings a person to the point of saying, "I have sinned." The surest sign that God is at work in his life is when he says that and means it. Anything less is simply sorrow for having made foolish mistakes—a reflex action caused by self-disgust.

The entrance into the kingdom of God is through the sharp, sudden pains of repentance colliding with man's respectable "goodness." Then the Holy Spirit, who produces these struggles, begins the formation of the Son of God in the person's life (see Galatians 4:19). This new life will reveal itself in conscious repentance followed by unconscious holiness, never the other way around. The foundation of Christianity is repentance. Strictly speaking, a person cannot repent when he chooses—repentance is a gift of God. The old Puritans used to pray for "the gift of tears." If you ever cease to understand the value of repentance, you allow yourself to remain in sin. Examine yourself to see if you have forgotten how to be truly repentant.[2]

Wow! Such incredible words!

After being shown the truth from the Word of God, I was then taken into this gut-wrenching experience of repentance. The Word of God says, "Godly sorrow produces repentance leading to salvation" (2 Cor. 7:10, NKJV). When the Word of God convicts us of what is wrong in our life, the godly sorrow is so all consuming that there is no other option but to repent of all the sins we have allowed ourselves to get caught up in *as believers*. We become horrified at what we have done and abhor the sins we have committed, which at the time we were committing them we may have felt were OK or even justified to do.

Godly sorrow forces us to face the fact and the reality that believers *do* sin and that God's Word has something to say about it. That is the purpose of this book. While going through this experience, I felt compelled to read all the scriptures to my husband and explain to him what I believed God was revealing to me. I suffer from a fear of reading out loud to other people; the words get all jumbled up like ants crawling across the page and I struggle to make sense of what I am trying to read.

But as I was reading each chapter and verse to my husband from Revelation 1:1 through 3:22, I read the words clearly and powerfully with no fear or anxiety. I felt as though God was speaking through me and giving me His strength and ability to do it. He wanted me to express to my husband the importance of His words in the Book of Revelation, and how, by and large, the churches are ignoring them and seem unaware that there are consequences to this.

In Revelation 1:20 Jesus refers to the seven churches to which the messages are written as "lampstands." Every church of Jesus Christ through history and throughout the world today is a lampstand. Let us take note here that Jesus' messages in the Book of Revelation are written to believers. In Revelation 2:5, Jesus says to the believers, "If you don't repent, I will come and remove your lampstand from its place among the churches."

The believers in the churches were doing things that Jesus warned them to repent of or He would "snuff them out" (my interpretation of removing a lampstand from its place among the churches). Many churches today are closing at an alarming rate or are at the very least ineffective within their communities. This applies not only to traditional churches who seem stuck in the rut of rituals that they may have practiced for centuries but also to relatively new churches that started out "on fire" for God but have somehow allowed sin to creep in through the door unchecked, unchallenged, and not repented of.

For example, the sin of pride will deceive churches into thinking they know how to run God's church without God's input. Other churches may bask in the "glory" of works they have accomplished in their communities and may repeat these apparent "successes" year after year. They build up a good reputation for themselves for what they are trying to achieve, even if their activities are bearing little fruit. This could give rise to the sin of desiring praise from others.

Whatever the situation may be, Jesus is trying to get the attention of His churches and particularly the shepherds (the leaders) of His flock. Jesus may even have to speak to

His leaders through the mouth of a fearful but courageous member of the flock. This may be a lady who makes the tea and coffee at the end of the service or a young adult who operates the media and resource desk who, despite their twenty-first century appearance, is also God's child and has ears and eyes wide open, ready to be used of God. We may be in a position of leadership in the church, but this does not mean we are the only people in the church that God has appointed to hear His voice.

As we are reminded several times in chapters 2 and 3 of Revelation, Jesus is speaking to "anyone with ears to hear." He has the sovereign right to use people who are not in leadership to speak to those who are in leadership if He is not able to get through to His leaders directly because of some sin within the church that may be blocking their ears from hearing.

When we ignore the Word of God being delivered to us by whatever means God chooses, we ignore it to our detriment. I would even go so far as to say that we ignore it at our peril, both personally and corporately as a church.

I feel very strongly that God is using the writing of this book to warn His church to *wake up* and that He wants to use the words of the Revelation of Jesus Christ to fulfill His will.

Chapter 2

THE PLEA

I WRITE THIS HUMBLY with my heart and soul to every single member of God's church on the face of the earth. I implore you to hear, listen, understand, and obey the words of Jesus Christ to His church. I am not writing this as someone who considers that they have got it all right and never puts a foot wrong. Such a Christian does not exist and will never exist, except in their own imagination.

I am writing this book from the position of my own failures, as a heart-wrenching plea from one who has committed many of the sins that Jesus Christ is confronting His churches with in the Book of Revelation. Not only did I commit many of these sins before Jesus saved me, which I know the blood of Christ washed away from me when He saved me, but the horrendous truth is that I have repeated many of these sins *since* He saved me. The reality of this fact is enormous, and many times the severity of it overwhelms me. How could I love my Lord so deeply, yet still allow myself to be blinded and deceived by Satan and enter into these sins, whatever the reason?

The Lord Jesus Christ is so merciful and gracious to have shown me in the Book of Revelation that when His churches are sinning (or individuals in the church are still sinning), He gives them time to repent and turn away from their sinful ways (see Rev. 2:21). The fact that Jesus

Christ, the Son of God, My Lord and Savior, is so loving, merciful, forgiving, and gracious that He is prepared to give me time to repent and turn away from the sins I am committing as a Christian, just blows me away. Rivers of tears have flowed from my eyes at receiving this truth from His Word.

However, as we will discover further in this book, with each of the warnings Jesus gives to His churches followed by His words of correction telling them what they must do to put things right, Jesus then warns them that if they refuse to repent and turn away from their sinful behavior (as Christians), He will bring consequences to bear upon their lives, which He describes in some detail.

This is serious. God takes sin within the church very seriously indeed; and as we will see, He clearly will not tolerate it. The consequences that will fall upon the church and individual believers for permitting sinful practices to remain within the church are far more serious than a daddy just saying to his misbehaving child that he will take away his sweets or his mobile phone for a week if he carries on disobeying him.

Since receiving this revelation, the weight of it inside me has felt enormous. I kept saying to God, "How can I possibly tell the global church of Jesus Christ in all its various forms that Jesus Christ Himself has a 'complaint' against them and that He is saying, 'I find that your actions do not meet the requirements of my God'" (Rev. 3:2)? I continued with my plea to God but felt He was already giving me His answer: He is trying to tell His church what the problems are through the Book of Revelation, so that He can give them time to repent and turn away from their sin, so that ultimately He does not have to bring such consequences into their lives.

I ask myself why anyone would believe what I write in this book. What credibility or authority do I have that would cause anyone to believe what I write? The only credibility I possess is that Jesus has revealed this to me. I have committed many of these sins as a Christian; and as such, from this humiliating position, I feel that He has given me His authority to voice His Word on this serious matter to His churches.

I feel compelled to do what He asks, and I lay this work upon His altar and trust Him with the outcome of it. I am one of His servants, just like every believer, just like the apostle John who wrote the Book of Revelation according to what Jesus Christ revealed to Him (Rev. 1:1–2).

I stress again that all believers are servants of God who He wants to use on this earth for His purposes and His glory. He wants us not only to preach the gospel to unbelievers but also to reveal the often hard truth of His Word to those who profess to be believers but are allowing themselves to be "entangled again with the yoke of bondage" (Gal. 5:1, KJV).

I believe that what Jesus is saying to His churches in the Book of Revelation is rarely heard from the pulpit. In fact I would go as far as to say that this very serious teaching has been greatly overlooked. It has been my experience that preachers and leaders seem reluctant to speak of these things for fear that they will lose their flock through such hard preaching. Many seem content to retain a "sickly" flock rather than determinedly deal with the sickness of sin that the sheep are engaging in and not repenting of.

It would appear that in many churches today there is a lukewarm and indifferent spirit in control. It waters down the truth of God's Word and keeps the flock in the fold with doctrine that has been altered by having the "rough edges" knocked off it. This makes it more palatable for the sheep to digest; the sheep are rarely given the opportunity to progress from the comforting "milk" of scripture to the life-transforming spiritual "meat" of tough but powerful doctrine.

As the writer to the Hebrews says:

> You have been believers so long now that you ought to be teaching others. Instead, you need someone to teach you again the basic things about God's word. You are like babies who need milk and cannot eat solid food. For someone who lives on milk is still an infant and doesn't know how to do what is right. Solid food is for those who are mature, who through training have the skills to recognize the difference between right and wrong.
> —HEBREWS 5:12–14

Church leaders may have full knowledge of these powerful, double-edged words of Jesus Christ, but Satan is the master of deception. It is highly likely that he has somehow managed to deceive leaders into believing that the flock doesn't need to hear the hard stuff. Satan will use phrases that sound really loving but are not the whole truth on the subject—phrases like "God is a God of love, He accepts us as we are." I have heard this used so often that I have lost count. It is an excuse to not have to acknowledge, face, and deal with the enormous pile of sin within the church that has been swept under the carpet for years. The pile under the carpet is so huge that everyone keeps tripping over it and even sweeping the dust off the top of it; but *no one* wants to deal with it. They may even put the church Christmas tree on top of it in an attempt to disguise it.

The preaching of the gospel is not meant to stop once

people are saved and have made it through the church door. The Word of God in all its fullness is meant to be taught to new and mature believers on an ongoing basis. It serves to show them how to live their everyday lives in Christ and for Christ. It tells them to hear and face the truth of what God has to say about sinning as a Christian and what to do about it when it occurs—the truth is, it *will* occur. Any gospel or doctrine that preaches otherwise is a false doctrine, a lie from Satan.

God doesn't say this to condemn us. This may sound strange to many, but God doesn't even condemn us when we have sinned as Christians (bear with me for the revelation on this). In fact, God is so gracious that when we fall into sin as Christians, He gives us time to repent and instructs us what to do to turn away from our sin. That would not be the action of a God who condemned us for sinning, would it? No! On the contrary, it is the result of God's amazing grace and love toward us. John tells a story that confirms this.

> Jesus returned to the Mount of Olives, but early the next morning he was back again at the Temple. A crowd soon gathered, and he sat down and taught them. As he was speaking, the teachers of religious law and the Pharisees brought a woman who had been caught in the act of adultery. They put her in front of the crowd. "Teacher," they said to Jesus, "this woman was caught in the act of adultery. The law of Moses says to stone her. What do you say?" They were trying to trap him into saying something they could use against him, but Jesus stooped down and wrote in the dust with his finger. They kept demanding an answer, so he stood up again and said, "All right, but let the one

who has never sinned throw the first stone!" Then
he stooped down again and wrote in the dust.
When the accusers heard this, they slipped away
one by one, beginning with the oldest, until only
Jesus was left in the middle of the crowd with
the woman. Then Jesus stood up again and said
to the woman, "Where are your accusers? Didn't
even one of them condemn you?" "No, Lord," she
said. And Jesus said, "Neither do I. Go and sin no
more."

—JOHN 8:1–11

So, here is the situation: we fall into sin and God shows
us His love by giving us time to repent and turn away
from sin and evil. But here is the hard-hitting reality: once
He has given us time to repent and turn away from our
sinful ways, if we refuse to do so, we are thereby declaring
that we prefer to love our sinful ways more than we love
Jesus—the One who died on the cross to save us from the
penalty of spending eternity in hell because of our sins. At
that point, the moment we choose to side with continuing
in sin despite the grace that God extends to us in giving
us time to repent as Christians, it is *our own* choice and
actions that bring the condemnation upon us. Notice that
the apostle Paul, in his letter to the Romans, says, "There
is therefore now no condemnation to them which are in
Christ Jesus, who walk not after the flesh, but after the
Spirit" (Rom. 8:1, KJV).

So, if we are in Christ Jesus but choose to walk after
the flesh, then our choices and actions bring condemnation upon us because of our disobedience and rebellion.
We cannot expect to live our lives "in Christ" any way we
want and think that there will not be any consequences.
This is childish wishful thinking.

Peter tells us:

> And when people escape from the wickedness of the world by knowing our Lord and Savior Jesus Christ and then get tangled up and enslaved by sin again, they are worse off than before. It would be better if they had never known the way to righteousness than to know it and then reject the command they were given to live a holy life. They prove the truth of this proverb: "A dog returns to its vomit." And another says, "A washed pig returns to the mud."
>
> —2 PETER 2:20–22

Luke also has a warning:

> When an evil spirit leaves a person, it goes into the desert, searching for rest. But when it finds none, it says, "I will return to the person I came from." So it returns and finds that its former home is all swept and in order. Then the spirit finds seven other spirits more evil than itself, and they all enter the person and live there. And so that person is worse off than before.
>
> —LUKE 11:24–26

Let me reiterate. God does not condemn us because we have fallen into sin. Condemnation comes upon us when we choose to reject what God has to say about sin, when we choose to reject His gracious gift of time to repent, when we choose to reject the amazing sacrifice of love He made for us through the shedding of the blood of His Son Jesus Christ upon the cross. And this rejection is evident when we choose and continue to live our lives in sinful ways in spite of the cross of Christ.

The truth is, we cannot carry on "turning a blind eye" to the huge and diverse forms of sin and evil that we are allowing to dwell in the church while we sit comfortably in the pews. As shocking as this may sound, I would not hesitate to say that every member of the global church of Jesus Christ has some form of sin or evil that they are allowing to remain in their lives unchecked. Some are huge and some are small; but all of it is sin, irrespective of its size. Many are not even aware of it, perhaps because they have been practicing a particular sin for so long that they have become used to its presence. They may have come to the place where Satan has deceived them into believing that what they are doing is not a sin but is part of their personality or part of their genetic makeup. This then leads us further into the sin of making excuses for our behavior when in fact what is needed is confession and repentance of our sin. We must allow the reality of the Cross of Christ to continually convict us of the sins we are allowing and excusing in our lives in order to bring us into repentance.

An excerpt from Oswald Chambers tells us:

> Never allow yourself to believe that Jesus Christ stands with us, and against God, out of pity or compassion, or that He became a curse for us out of sympathy for us. Jesus Christ became a curse for us by divine decree. Our part in realising the tremendous meaning of His curse is the conviction of sin. Conviction is given to us as a gift of shame and repentance; it is the great mercy of God. Jesus Christ hates the sin in people and Calvary is the measure of His hatred.[1]

I believe that we need to be living our lives daily with a repentant spirit. As Jesus could come back at any moment, when we least expect it, we really need to be repenting every second of every day, of every week, of every month, and of every year of all the things we think, say, feel, and do that are not in keeping with the Word of God. This may seem like an overexaggeration. But since going through a tremendous ordeal in order to be able to write this book to fulfill God's purpose and to give Him the glory, I now believe that the Lord really does want His children to have hearts toward Him that are desperate to confess their daily sins to Him and receive His forgiveness and cleansing from all their unrighteousness. The peace and liberation that comes from this level of relationship with the Lord is beyond description.

The Word of God ultimately puts the responsibility of the spiritual condition of the body of Christ (the church), corporately and individually, firmly and squarely on the shoulders of the leaders. If leaders are allowing sins to dwell in the church and not exposing them to the light of Christ and the truth of His Word, the longer this goes on the worse it will get. Then sadly another "lampstand" is removed from its place among the churches. For leaders to do nothing about it is, in effect, condoning sin. They cannot use the excuse that they didn't know it existed in their church. It exists in every church.

The leaders are God's shepherds of the flock; and He has appointed them to care for the sheep and to be on the lookout for signs of disease, "parasites," and whatever is ailing the sheep. They then need to do whatever is necessary to clean the flock and restore them to full health and full life.

The great responsibility of revealing the truth of the Revelation of Jesus Christ to the individual members of the church lies upon the shoulders of those He has appointed to be leaders. They neglect this awesome, holy privilege at enormous cost to themselves and their sheep. As Jesus says, "They are blind guides leading the blind, and if one blind person guides another, they will both fall into a ditch" (Matt. 15:14).

If the shepherds will not lead the sheep in accordance with the *entirety* of the holy Word of God and will not reveal the truth of the Book of Revelation to their church members, then each individual member needs to grasp hold of this responsibility for themselves. They need to pray for God to lead them to the right people and the right Christian resources that will help them to learn and grow in the ways of the Lord. We need to be proactive in our search for Christian groups, services, meetings, events, and seminars that teach about the sins we struggle with as a Christian. Then we need to follow through by making ourselves accountable to another Christian of the same gender who is mature enough in their faith to handle what we may have to disclose to them and strong enough to challenge us with difficult questions. The purpose and goal is to break free from these sins we habitually fall into. We need to stop making excuses for them—some to the point that we give up trying with a sigh of resignation saying, "I can't help it; it's just the way I am. I am not strong enough to overcome it." Such talk is a lie from Satan from the depths of hell. We need to grasp the reality that we are caught up in a battle for our souls, a fierce battle raging in the heavens.

We need to shape up, polish our spiritual boots, and be ready with our full armor in Christ on, ready to fend off every fiery dart of the evil one. We need to walk forward confidently with the shoes of the gospel upon our feet, with the belt of truth of the Word of God tied firmly around our waist, with the breastplate of the righteousness of God secured firmly over our body, with the helmet of the knowledge of the truth of our salvation fitted firmly on our heads. We need to protect ourselves with the shield of our faith in Jesus Christ and wield the powerful double-edged sword of the Spirit, which is the Holy Word of God (see Ephesians 6:10–18). All demons including Satan himself will flee and must flee when we use the Word of the Lord God Almighty in the authority and name of Jesus Christ. We must be ready night and day for every attack of the evil one. Make no mistake, this will continue until the last trump shall sound.

How can we be ready if we not only neglect to put our armor on but even neglect to look after it? Do we just toss the whole armor of God out of sight into the corner of some room, shut the door, and leave the precious armor that God has given to us to wear and use to gather dust and dirt?

Our leaders cannot make us put our armor on or make us take care of it. They can instruct us to do so; but sadly many leaders do not even realize that they need to do it themselves. Let us pray for all leaders to be people of God who will step up to the mark and lead their flock boldly and courageously. Pray for all leaders to teach the flock the truth of the double-edged, powerful words of the only true Shepherd, Jesus Christ. Jesus' will is that the flock be made "holy and clean, washed by the cleansing of God's Word, [and] to present the flock to Himself as a glorious church without spot or wrinkle or any other blemish. Instead, she will be holy and without fault" (Eph. 5:26–27). Therefore, let us take the revelation of Jesus Christ to His churches *seriously.*

If the shepherds *only* tell the flock of the wonderful life that awaits them in heaven, as described in various passages in chapters 4 through 22 of the Book of Revelation, then they are misleading the flock by the sin of omission. It is absolutely essential that the shepherds tell the flock *all* that Jesus is saying to all His churches in the letters to the churches in chapters 2 and 3 of Revelation. This cannot and must not be ignored.

How we live our life on earth as Christians determines our eternal outcome. We surely cannot presume that all of the blessings of the kingdom of God in heaven will be ours, regardless of how we live our lives in Christ on this earth.

We must remind ourselves continually that Jesus' messages in Revelation are written to believers; and so each time He refers to the sexually immoral, the idolaters, the murderers, the thieves, etc., He is talking about Christians who are still sinning within the church.

From the scriptures in the Book of Revelation, we will see that Jesus says that any believer who falls into sin but then repents of their evil sin and turns back to Christ and overcomes their sin will enter the kingdom of God. We know from scriptures in the New Testament that Jesus says all unbelievers will end up in hell. By the use of the words "all unbelievers," this must imply both "good" unbelievers and "bad" unbelievers. Anyone who does not have Jesus Christ as their Lord and Savior is deemed an unbeliever and will dwell for eternity in hell where they will be tormented night and day, forever. They refused to put their faith in Jesus while they were given the opportunity to do so. Being good and doing good on this earth is not a ticket into heaven.

Faith in Jesus Christ is the only way to be saved—no other name in heaven or on earth will save us. "There is salvation in no one else! God has given no other name under heaven by which we must be saved" (Acts 4:12). But once we are saved, the Word of God instructs us to "work hard to show the results of your salvation, obeying God with deep reverence and fear" (Phil. 2:12).

The fire of eternal hell is for all unbelievers whether they are good or bad unbelievers. The *full* blessings of heaven are for those who are believers who have repentant hearts and teachable spirits, who hunger and thirst after righteousness, who choose to confess their sins, and who turn away from any sinful practices they have fallen into in their journey as a Christian. Accordingly, what then is the eternal place of believers who keep on sinning and who refuse to repent of their sinful practices, despite being warned by the Son of God to do so? Surely their eternal fate cannot be the same as continually repentant believers? Surely any believer who refuses to obey the words of their Savior Jesus Christ is living a lie?

Jesus is speaking to *believers* in the following three scriptures:

> Look, I will come unexpectedly as a thief! Blessed are all who are watching for me, who keep their clothing ready so they will not have to walk around naked and ashamed.
>
> —Revelation 16:15

> Blessed are those who wash their robes. They will be permitted to enter through the gates of the city and eat the fruit from the tree of life. Outside the city are the dogs—the sorcerers, the sexually immoral, the murderers, the idol worshipers, and all who love to live a lie.
>
> —Revelation 22:14–15

> And I solemnly declare to everyone who hears
> the words of the prophecy written in this book:
> If anyone adds anything to what is written here,
> God will add to that person the plagues described
> in this book. And if anyone removes any of the
> words from this book of prophecy [i.e., water it
> down, not preach the whole truth, deny that Jesus'
> messages need to be applied today, etc.], God will
> remove that person's share in the tree of life and
> in the holy city that are described in this book.
> —REVELATION 22:18–19

These scriptures clearly inform us that Christians who refuse to repent of their continual sinful practices will not be permitted to enter the city gates or share in the tree of life. Revelation 16:15 tells us that these Christians who are not "ready" when Jesus returns will walk around naked and ashamed. Revelation 22:15 informs us that such believers will be left outside the city gates.

They may not end up in hell with unbelievers who are practicing the same sins. But it is clear that Christians who refuse to repent of the sins they enjoy indulging in will not be permitted to enter the city and will walk around naked and ashamed outside the gates. Could this suggest the existence of some sort of barren place between the gates of hell and the gates of heaven reserved for disobedient believers who refuse to listen to and obey the Word of God?

They may be saved from hell simply because they believe in Jesus Christ. But because their lives are not lived in such a way that glorifies and honors Him, they will never inherit the blessings that are laid up for those believers who live their lives on earth in obedience to His Word. These believers are living each day trusting in the power and strength of the Lord, continually repenting to the best of their ability of the sins they commit, whether knowingly or ignorantly.

To be saved from the fires of hell but only to find yourself walking around naked and ashamed *outside* the city gates is literally being saved by the "skin of your teeth." They are saved from eternal torment but spend eternity in shame outside the city gates for willfully disobeying the words of Jesus. In one ear they would hear the eternal torment of those in hell while in the other ear hearing the eternal joy, rejoicing, and worship of those who have entered the city gates through believing and obeying the Words of Jesus to His churches. Jesus has not given us these messages for nothing. The eternal state of every believer hangs on Jesus' every word.

If you feel that what I am writing is nonsense or even "false teaching," please read the following passages of Scripture containing words from the mouth of Jesus Himself:

> [Jesus said,] "Not everyone who calls out to me, 'Lord! Lord!' will enter the Kingdom of Heaven. Only those who actually do the will of my Father in heaven will enter. On judgment day many will say to me, 'Lord! Lord! We prophesied in your name and cast out demons in your name and performed many miracles in your name.' But I will reply, 'I never knew you. Get away from me, you who break God's laws.'"
> —MATTHEW 7:21–23

> [Jesus said,] "Be dressed for service and keep your lamps burning, as though you were waiting for your master to return from the wedding feast. Then you will be ready to open the door and let

him in the moment he arrives and knocks. The servants who are ready and waiting for His return will be rewarded. I tell you the truth, he himself will seat them, put on an apron, and serve them as they sit and eat! He may come in the middle of the night or just before dawn. But whenever He comes, He will reward the servants who are ready. Understand this: If a homeowner knew exactly when a burglar was coming, he would not permit his house to be broken into. You also must be ready all the time, for the Son of Man will come when least expected."

Peter asked, "Lord, is that illustration just for us or for everyone?" And the Lord replied, "A faithful, sensible servant is one to whom the master can give the responsibility of managing his other household servants and feeding them. If the master returns and finds that the servant has done a good job, there will be a reward. I tell you the truth, the master will put that servant in charge of all he owns. But what if the servant thinks, 'My master won't be back for a while,' and he begins beating the other servants, partying, and getting drunk? The master will return unannounced and unexpected, and he will cut the servant in pieces and banish him with the unfaithful. And a servant who knows what the master wants, but isn't prepared and doesn't carry out those instructions, will be severely punished."

—LUKE 12:35–47

Jesus said, "There was a certain rich man who was splendidly clothed in purple and fine linen and who lived each day in luxury. At his gate lay a poor man named Lazarus who was covered with sores. As Lazarus lay there longing for scraps from the rich man's table, the dogs would come and lick his open sores. Finally, the poor man died and was carried by the angels to be with Abraham. The rich man also died and was buried, and his soul went to the place of the dead. There, in torment, he saw Abraham in the far distance with Lazarus at his side. The rich man shouted, 'Father Abraham, have some pity! Send Lazarus over here to dip the tip of his finger in water and cool my tongue. I am in anguish in these flames.'

"But Abraham said to him, 'Son, remember that during your lifetime you had everything you wanted, and Lazarus had nothing. So now he is here being comforted, and you are in anguish. And besides, there is a great chasm separating us. No one can cross over to you from here, and no one can cross over to us from there.' Then the rich man said, 'Please, Father Abraham, at least send him to my father's home. For I have five brothers, and I want him to warn them so they don't end up in this place of torment.' But Abraham said, 'Moses and the prophets have warned them. Your brothers can read what they wrote.' The rich man replied, 'No, Father Abraham! But if someone is sent to them from the dead, then they will repent of their sins and turn to God.' But Abraham said, 'If they won't listen to Moses and the prophets, they won't listen even if someone rises from the dead.'"

—Luke 16:19–31

[Jesus said,] "Then the Kingdom of Heaven will be like ten bridesmaids who took their lamps and went to meet the bridegroom. Five of them were foolish, and five were wise. The five who were foolish didn't take enough olive oil for their lamps, but the other five were wise enough to take along extra oil. When the bridegroom was delayed, they all became drowsy and fell asleep. At midnight they were roused by the shout, 'Look, the bridegroom is coming! Come out and meet him!' All the bridesmaids got up and prepared their lamps. Then the five foolish ones asked the others, 'Please give us some of your oil because our lamps are going out.' But the others replied, 'We don't have enough for all of us. Go to a shop and buy some for yourselves.' But while they were gone to buy oil, the bridegroom came. Then those who were ready went in with him to the marriage feast, and the door was locked. Later, when the other five bridesmaids returned, they stood outside, calling, 'Lord! Lord! Open the door for us!' But he called back, 'Believe me, I don't know you!' So you, too, must keep watch! For you do not know the day or hour of my return."

—MATTHEW 25:1–13

Jesus went through the towns and villages, teaching as he went, always pressing on toward Jerusalem. Someone asked him, "Lord, will only a few be saved?" He replied, "Work hard to enter the narrow door to God's Kingdom, for many will try to enter but will fail. When the master of the house has locked the door, it will be too late. You will stand outside knocking and pleading, 'Lord, open the door for us!' But he will reply, 'I don't know you or where you come from.' Then you will say, 'But we ate and drank with you, and you taught in our streets.' And he will reply, 'I tell you,

I don't know you or where you come from. Get away from me, all you who do evil.'

"There will be weeping and gnashing of teeth, for you will see Abraham, Isaac, Jacob, and all the prophets in the Kingdom of God, but you will be thrown out. And people will come from all over the world—from east and west, north and south—to take their places in the Kingdom of God. And note this: Some who seem least important now will be the greatest then, and some who are the greatest now will be least important then."

—LUKE 13:22–30

[Jesus said,] "Two men will be working together in the field; one will be taken, the other left. Two women will be grinding flour at the mill; one will be taken, the other left. So you, too, must keep watch! For you don't know what day your Lord is coming. Understand this: If a homeowner knew exactly when a burglar was coming, he would keep watch and not permit his house to be broken into. You also must be ready all the time, for the Son of Man will come when least expected.

"A faithful, sensible servant is one to whom the master can give the responsibility of managing his other household servants and feeding them. If the master returns and finds that the servant has done a good job, there will be a reward. I tell you the truth, the master will put that servant in charge of all he owns. But what if the servant is evil and thinks, 'My master won't be back for a while,' and he begins beating the other servants, partying, and getting drunk? The master will return unannounced and unexpected, and he will cut the servant to pieces and assign him a place with the hypocrites. In that place there will be weeping and gnashing of teeth."

—MATTHEW 24:40–51

These passages confirm that not every believer will actually enter the gates to the city, the kingdom of heaven. Many will be refused entry based on the way they lived their lives as believers while on earth. They will remain outside the gates, where there will be weeping and gnashing of teeth. I firmly believe that if they were going to end up in hell, Jesus would have actually said so in these passages rather than using the words "outside the city gates."

Jesus doesn't say that they will end up in hell but clearly says that they will not enter the gates of heaven and will remain outside the gates where there will be weeping and gnashing of teeth. This could suggest that the souls of disobedient and rebellious Christians may be saved from eternal torment in hell but will not be permitted to enter the kingdom of heaven or enjoy its blessings. These things are the right and the inheritance of believers who have made themselves ready and continually keep themselves ready day and night, watching and waiting for the return of the Lord.

If we get caught up in the ways of the world while we are waiting for His return—pleasing ourselves, partying, and socializing too much—and put our prayer life, our Bible study, and our relationship with God on the back burner, we are like the person who built their house without a foundation and are in serious danger of coming to ruin.

So why do you keep calling me "Lord, Lord!" when you don't do what I say? I will show you what it's like when someone comes to me, listens to my teaching, and then follows it. It is like a person building a house who digs deep and lays the foundation on solid rock. When the floodwaters rise and break against that house, it stands firm because it is well built. But anyone who hears and doesn't obey is like a person who builds a house without a foundation. When the floods sweep down against that house, it will collapse into a heap of ruins.

—LUKE 6:46–49

The writer of Hebrews says:

Be careful you do not refuse to listen to the one who is speaking. For if the people of Israel did not escape when they refused to listen to Moses, the earthly messenger, we will certainly not escape if we reject the one who speaks to us from heaven!

—HEBREWS 25:12

Further, in verses 28–29, he wrote:

Since we are receiving a Kingdom that is unshakeable, let us be thankful and please God by worshiping him with holy fear and awe. For our God is a devouring fire.

Let's cut to the chase here: how many churches, leaders, and individual members are currently "living a lie," and are not willing to admit it or confess it, let alone repent of it or turn away from it? How many leaders are in effect "removing" great chunks of the words of the Book of the Revelation of Jesus Christ by not preaching and teaching the church about its *whole* message due to fear, unbelief, indifference, or whatever the reason?

When are we going to take the words of Jesus Christ seriously?

When are we going to take *Jesus* seriously?

Chapter 3

WHERE DO WE GO FROM HERE?

W HAT FOLLOWS IN chapters 4 through 10 of this book is what I feel God has revealed and spoken to me about. He wants me to relate Jesus' messages to the churches (indeed, *every* church) from the Book of Revelation of Jesus Christ chapters 2 and 3.

When these were revealed to me, I experienced extremely heavy conviction of the sins in my own life; sins that I was allowing to dwell in me and making excuses for. The conviction of the Holy Spirit was so intense that I could not stop crying for several days. I felt deep shame and utter brokenness that I had behaved with such appalling disregard toward God and all that Jesus' death on the cross cost Him for my sake.

What I will be writing in these chapters is not intended to "add" to what is already written in the Book of Revelation; neither is there any intention of "removing" anything from it. The purpose of my writing is to draw attention to what is or may be dwelling in the churches today, infecting them and slowly destroying them, like a silent deadly killer disease. This grieves the heart of our Savior, Jesus Christ. This is why He has shown and is showing His church just how much He loves us by pointing out to us what is wrong and instructing us how to put it right.

My prayer is that we will individually (as members of

the church) and corporately (as the global church of Jesus Christ) experience the loving but firm hand of the Lord pressing down upon us as He touches us with His mighty, convicting Holy Spirit. May this cause us to fall to our knees in complete brokenness for what we have thought we could get away with, deceiving ourselves with such thoughts as "It's in secret, nobody knows," or, "It's not hurting anyone." What lies from the pit of hell those are!

Our secret sins may not *appear* to be hurting anyone on earth, but they are most definitely hurting and grieving our Father in heaven. Every time we do whatever it is that we *know* is not in keeping with our holy God, we are in effect spitting in the face of our Savior Jesus Christ. Our continual and unrepentant sinning is basically saying to Him: "Thanks, Jesus! It's really nice of You to die for me, to have Your body mutilated for me, and to have Your blood shed for me. I hope You don't mind but I love what I am doing so much that I am going to carry on doing it. I know it is an abomination to You, but I actually like it and don't intend to give it up for anybody, not even You, Jesus."

Let's think about it in a more personal way. Let's say we do something kind, generous, and sacrificial for someone and they don't show much of a response or even no response at all—not even a thank you. Then they seem to carry on behaving in the same old ways as if we had not even done something kind, generous, and sacrificial for them. How does their lack of response make us feel? In our natural self, we would probably feel really hurt and think to ourselves, *How ungrateful!* We may feel aggrieved; perhaps anger rises up inside us. We may even not want to associate with them anymore and may resort to crossing them off our Christmas card list.

If this is how we feel about other people's gross

ingratitude to our gifts of love to them, how much more must our Savior feel about it when we continually convince ourselves that it is acceptable to carry on indulging in our sinful practices, disregarding His gift of love to us?

May we now, as the church of Jesus Christ, confess our individual and corporate sins to each other and to our heavenly Father, thereby bringing them out of darkness and into the glorious light of Christ. Let us then come to a place of deep repentance and turn away fully from everything that we are doing, saying, thinking, and feeling that is grieving the Father, Son, and Holy Spirit. Let us also repent of our gross sin of ungratefulness for the sacrifice of love for us on the cross. I am certain that we have no idea just how enormous this sin of ungratefulness is when viewed from God's perspective.

We need to look at *all* of our continual sinful practices, behaviors, attitudes, and thoughts from *God's* perspective in relation to the crucifixion of His Son on the cross. Every time we, as Christians, continue to choose to do our "sinful thing," we are effectively hammering another nail into Jesus' body. Didn't the weight of the sin of the world cause Him to suffer enough agony the first time around? As believers, must we continue to keep torturing and mutilating our Savior over and over again with our refusal to repent of our continual deeds of darkness?

It is time for change in the house of God; time for ridding it of all that pollutes and defiles it; time to cleanse it and purify it; time to put right what is wrong; time for conflicts to be resolved and relationships to be reconciled, healed, and restored. It is time for the church to wake up and present herself as the beautiful, glorious, spotless bride of Christ. The witness of Jesus Christ in us to the world is at stake if we choose to ignore the stains of unrepentant sinful behavior that are covering our wedding garment.

Yes, the shed blood of Jesus has pardoned us and forgiven us of the sins we committed before coming to Christ, *and* His shed blood continues to pardon and forgive us of the sins we commit "in-Christ"—*if* we confess them to Him. This is confirmed by the apostle John when he says to believers:

> If we say we have no sin, we deceive ourselves, and the truth is not in us. If we confess our sins, He is faithful and just to forgive us our sins, and to cleanse us from all unrighteousness.
>
> —1 JOHN 1:8–9, KJV

It is clear from this verse that *we* have the responsibility here, as John used the word *if.* God is saying that *if we* confess our sins, then *He* is faithful and just to forgive us of our sins and to cleanse us from all unrighteousness.

But, *if* we *don't* or *won't* confess our sins; *if* we *don't* or *won't* repent and turn away from our sinful thoughts, feelings, words, and actions; what then? Are we really so deceived that we would convince ourselves that there are no consequences to unconfessed and unrepentant sin? That is the attitude of the *"whatever"* culture that we live in; a culture that rejects any form of authority or discipline, the reality of right and wrong, and the purpose of boundaries and consequences.

The apostle Paul in his letter to the Galatians says,

> Don't be misled—you cannot mock the justice of God. You will always harvest what you plant. Those who live only to satisfy their own sinful nature will harvest decay and death from that

sinful nature. But those who live to please the
Spirit will harvest everlasting life from the Spirit.
                                    —GALATIANS 6:7–8

This was spoken to believers, but many Christians hold
the mistaken belief that this just applies to unbelievers.
Many Christians believe that because they are now "in-
Christ," there is no longer any consequence for continued
sinful behavior as a believer. Because we are "in Christ"
do we really think that we are above this eternal law of
God? We know this law better as "you reap what you sow,"
and we are very quick to use it to judge people of the
world who are *not* in Christ. We say, "They get what they
deserve," which is the same as saying, "You reap what you
sow" (see Gal. 6:9).

I would suggest that God holds believers even more
responsible and accountable to this truth from His Word.
When Jesus says in Revelation 3:2, "I find that your actions
do not meet the requirements of my God," it is clear that
when God saved us through our faith in Jesus Christ, He
put within us His standards of life. If we walk in the light
of the truth of His Word and allow the Holy Spirit to
work in us according to the will of God, the work He has
started within us He will complete (Phil. 1:6). But this is
if we remain in submission to His authority and His lord-
ship over our lives.

God's standards are not the world's standards. They are
contrary to the ways of the world. And as such, we fight
and struggle against them when the Holy Spirit is trying
to expose them to us and to challenge us to confess, repent,
and turn away from them. He encourages us to begin to
live our lives in accordance with His standards, so that
our actions begin to come into line with the requirements

of God. His will is for us to obey Him out of our love for His Son Jesus Christ. Jesus says, "If you love me, keep my commandments" (John 14:15, KJV).

In our earthly relationships, if we say we love someone, our actions will demonstrate this. If we say we love someone but our actions toward them show that we don't like what they are asking of us and we proceed to rebel against their requests, then we really only love ourselves and what we want. Our love for them is false and is only based on what we can get *from* the other person. It is a distorted form of love rooted in selfishness.

It is the same with our love for God. We cannot say we love God if our relationship with Him is based solely on what we want Him to do for us. We cannot say we love God if we refuse to accept the fact and the reality that *our* obedience to what He says and what He requires *of us* is the major part of our continued relationship and fellowship with Him.

It is not optional; it is essential! Our spiritual lives depend on it.

> So we are lying if we say we have fellowship with
> God but go on living in spiritual darkness; we are
> not practicing the truth.
>
> —1 JOHN 1:6

God leaves the choice—the decision, firmly with us. He makes His standard very clear so that we are left without excuse. Oswald Chambers tells us, "If my relationship to Him is that of love, I will do what He says without hesitation….Jesus Christ will not force me to obey Him, but I must."[1]

We must face the reality of God's verdict of sin and

no longer make provision for it or excuses for it in our lives. We must willingly let God make us holy, and that means exposing all that is deep within us. Only then can the Holy Spirit truly continue His work of making us holy and spotless and without blemish as the purified bride of Christ.

We must no longer sulk around like selfish children, stomping our feet because we want to carry on being "naughty children," when in fact it is time to grow up. If the church doesn't wake up and become a place where the sheep can expose the dirt and mess of their lives and be helped to become clean and purified of the defilement of the sins that they have allowed to remain in their lives, there is nowhere else for them to go, is there? As hard as it sounds and as much as we don't like it and continually fight against it and find ways of evading and avoiding our responsibility, God's Word tells us that judgment begins with the house of God. Following are several scriptures that confirm this:

> For the time has come for judgment, and it must begin with God's household. And if judgment begins with us, what terrible fate awaits those who have never obeyed God's Good News?
>
> —1 Peter 4:17

> For the time is come that judgment must begin at the house of God: and if it first begin at us, what shall the end be of them that obey not the gospel of God?
>
> —1 Peter 4:17, kjv

> Dear friends, if we deliberately continue sinning after we have received knowledge of the truth,

there is no longer any sacrifice that will cover these sins. There is only the terrible expectation of God's judgment and the raging fire that will consume his enemies. For anyone who refused to obey the law of Moses was put to death without mercy on the testimony of two or three witnesses. Just think how much worse the punishment will be for those who have trampled on the Son of God, and have treated the blood of the covenant, which made us holy, as if it were common and unholy, and have insulted and disdained the Holy Spirit who brings God's mercy to us. For we know the one who said, "I will take revenge. I will pay them back." He also said, "The LORD will judge his own people." It is a terrible thing to fall into the hands of the living God.

—HEBREWS 10:26–31

And you must show mercy to those whose faith is wavering. Rescue others by snatching them from the flames of judgment. Show mercy to still others, but do so with great caution, hating the sins that contaminate their lives.

—JUDE 22–23

Dear brothers and sisters, if another believer is overcome by some sin, you who are godly should gently and humbly help that person back onto the right path. And be careful not to fall into the same temptation yourself.

—GALATIANS 6:1

Let there be no sexual immorality, impurity, or greed among you. Such sins have no place among God's people. Obscene stories, foolish talk, and coarse jokes—these are not for you. Instead, let there be thankfulness to God. You can be sure that no immoral, impure, or greedy person will inherit the Kingdom of Christ and of God. For a greedy person is an idolater, worshiping the things of this world.

Don't be fooled by those who try to excuse these sins, for the anger of God will fall on all who disobey him. Don't participate in the things these people do. For once you were full of darkness, but now you have light from the Lord. So live as people of light! For this light within you produces only what is good and right and true. Carefully determine what pleases the Lord. Take no part in the worthless deeds of evil and darkness; instead, expose them. It is shameful even to talk about the things that ungodly people do in secret. But their evil intentions will be exposed when the light shines on them, for the light makes everything visible. This is why it is said, "Awake, O sleeper, rise up from the dead, and Christ will give you light."

So be careful how you live. Don't live like fools, but like those who are wise. Make the most of every opportunity in these evil days. Don't act thoughtlessly, but understand what the Lord wants you to do. Don't be drunk with wine, because that will ruin your life. Instead, be filled with the Holy Spirit, singing psalms and hymns and spiritual songs among yourselves, and making music to the Lord in your hearts. And give thanks for everything to God the Father in the name of our Lord Jesus Christ.

—EPHESIANS 5:3–20

> My dear brothers and sisters, if someone among
> you wanders away from the truth and is brought
> back, you can be sure that whoever brings the
> sinner back will save that person from death and
> bring about the forgiveness of many sins.
>
> —JAMES 5:19–20

The Word of God also says that the shepherds (the church leaders) have the responsibility of watching out for the souls of their flock. This is an awesome responsibility given to them by God. It ought to be undertaken with fear and trembling to ensure that the body of believers is taught and instructed in accordance with the *entire* Word of God, without compromise or deviation.

> Obey your spiritual leaders, and do what they say.
> Their work is to watch over your souls, and they
> are accountable to God. Give them reason to do
> this with joy and not with sorrow. That would
> certainly not be for your benefit.
>
> —HEBREWS 13:17

So, if judgment begins with the house of God and the shepherds are held accountable for the spiritual welfare of the flock, then may we all—shepherds and sheep—fall on our knees with reverential fear of almighty God. Let us repent of our blasé and irreverent attitude toward God and His Word.

Let's get real here. He is almighty God who holds the power of life and death in His hands. He has the power to raise up churches and the power to remove them. This should literally strike the fear of God in us. We must stop playing games with God!

So, now it really is time. Come on Church! Wake up!

MESSAGES FROM THE BOOK OF REVELATION

THE FIRST THING we need to note and fully comprehend is that Jesus' messages in the Book of Revelation are *His* words and instructions *to believers* in the churches. These messages were given by Jesus *after* He had ascended into heaven following His crucifixion, burial, and resurrection. Jesus is clearly watching what is going on within the churches *from* the heavenly realm, where He is at the right hand of His Father—Almighty God.

While the messages in the Book of Revelation are titled to the seven churches in the cities of Ephesus, Smyrna, Pergamum, Thyatira, Sardis, Philadelphia, and Laodicea, I believe that the Lord is revealing that the messages are not only for them but for all churches for all time until Jesus' second coming.

Jesus says, "Anyone with ears to hear *must* listen to the Spirit *and* understand what He is saying to *the churches*" (Rev. 2:7, 11, 17; 3:6, 13, 22, emphasis added). The fact that Jesus says this so many times to believers—the churches, is evidence to me that Jesus means precisely what He says. He repeats it over and over again to hammer the message home: "This is important! Do something before it is too late!"

As we have seen earlier from many scriptures, it is highly possible that believers who are not repentant of their sinful behavior, who are generally disobedient to the Word of God, or who are halfhearted in their walk may find that they are not permitted to enter into the kingdom of heaven. They may find themselves outside the gates, unable to enjoy the presence of the Lord, only able to hear the endless worship from the outside. Imagine being in that desolate and desperate place, walking around naked and ashamed (Rev. 16:15) for eternity because we failed to take God's Word seriously and thought we could just pick the bits we like but ignore the tough stuff in His Word.

We may have been saved by the skin of our teeth from being thrown into the pit of hell simply because at some point in our life we did turn to Christ and believed in Him as the Son of God and our Lord and Savior. But somewhere along the way we fell back into our sinful ways and ignored all God's warnings, preferring to love our sins more than we love Jesus. The price we may have to pay for our refusal to repent is eternity *outside* the kingdom of heaven.

Many times in the New Testament—the Gospels, the Epistles, and the Book of Revelation—we are told that if we continually sin as believers and refuse to repent of these sins, we will not enter the kingdom of heaven. I am staggered that we have missed this truth. It is there for us all to see, but Satan has blinded our eyes to it. We have just assumed that Jesus, and the apostles in their letters, were talking about *unbelievers* not getting into the kingdom of heaven because of their sins.

I have been a Christian for twenty years, and I have to confess that I have failed to see this truth. I thank God that He has now revealed it to me so that I can reveal this truth to you, for God's purpose and glory.

Can you believe that Satan is capable of making believers "assume" that they are going to enter the gates of heaven regardless of their ongoing, ungodly, unrepentant behavior? What a shocking deception! This is not what God's Word says, and we have seen this from the scriptures I have shared already in this book.

Jesus will now reveal this truth to us again as we embark on the study of His letters to the churches from the Book of

Revelation. Let us read His Word with a prayerful, humble, and teachable spirit. If we continue to ignore Jesus' warnings, we are in effect playing "Russian Roulette" with our eternal destiny. If we continue to walk in sin, disobedience, and rebellion against God's Word; and if we refuse to be convicted of sin and choose not to repent and turn away from these things; then the tragedy is that *we* will be the losers in this dangerous game we have played against God.

Let us begin looking at what Jesus is saying to every believer in every church throughout the world.

> Then a cloud overshadowed them, and a voice from the cloud said, "This is my dearly loved Son. Listen to him."
>
> —MARK 9:7

(See also Matthew 17:5; Luke 9:35.)

Chapter 4

THE MESSAGE OF JESUS CHRIST
TO THE CHURCH IN EPHESUS

Write this letter to the angel of the church in Ephesus. This is the message from the one who holds the seven stars in His right hand, the one who walks among the seven gold lampstands: I know all the things you do. I have seen your hard work and your patient endurance. I know you don't tolerate evil people. You have examined the claims of those who say they are apostles but are not. You have discovered they are liars. You have patiently suffered for me without quitting. But I have this complaint against you. You don't love me or each other as you did at first! Look how far you have fallen! Turn back to me and do the works you did at first. If you don't repent, I will come and remove your lampstand from its place among the churches. But this is in your favor: you hate the evil deeds of the Nicolaitans, just as I do. Anyone with ears to hear must listen to the Spirit and understand what he is saying to the churches. To everyone who is victorious I will give fruit from the tree of life in the paradise of God.

—REVELATION 2:1–7

L ET US RECALL that earlier on I mentioned that Jesus refers to His churches as "lampstands," and in Revelation 2:1 above He says that He walks among the lampstands. This means that He is there in all of our churches hearing and seeing everything that we do or don't do, as the case may be.

So as we begin studying this message of Jesus Christ to the church in Ephesus, immediately we can see that Jesus has noticed that the church is working hard, is patiently enduring, and *doesn't* tolerate evil people. The church has examined and exposed people who have claimed to be apostles and discovered them to be liars. Jesus is pleased with all of this, including patiently enduring suffering for Him and not giving up. At a quick glance, this church appears to be doing really well; Jesus praises them for all of this.

But then Jesus says, "But I have this complaint against you" (v. 4). Here is a great church doing great things. The Creator of all things praises them openly, exalting them for their determination to walk in His ways. But does Jesus just give them a nice pat on the back and turn a blind eye to a problem He can see? *No!* He confronts them with it— with no messing around, no mincing His words, and no watering it down. He gives it to them in plain and simple terms. What is His complaint against this church?

> You don't love me or others as you did at first! Look how far you have fallen! Turn back to me and do the works you did at first. If you don't repent, I will come and remove your lampstand from its place among the churches.
>
> —REVELATION 2:4–5

This is serious! Jesus is saying in effect, "If you don't get your act together and show your love for Me by loving each other the way you used to when you first believed— in the sacrificial way that I have loved you—then I will cause your church to be snuffed out; it will no longer exist."

This surely is a warning to every church. Jesus requires us to love one another with His sacrificial love; putting the needs of others before our own. It is clear that Jesus can see a spirit of selfishness and conditional halfhearted love dwelling within the church. But the church is so into "good works" that they are neglecting to check in regularly with how they are loving and treating one another. Jesus says that if they don't open their eyes, repent of their neglect and deal with it, and completely change their ways, such neglect will be enough for *Him* to remove the church from its place among churches.

Jesus does finish the message with another word of encouragement by saying "But this is in your favor, you hate the evil deeds of the Nicolaitans, just as I do" (v. 6).

Note this: Jesus' initial praise of this church and His final encouragement to them *does not* cancel out His confrontation of the sin within the church and His stern warning to repent of it. All too often churches today have a major focus on what is good and worthy of praise and encouragement, which is good and very much needed. But this should not be at the exclusion of confronting and dealing with the evil deeds of darkness that lurk in every corner. It is clear from Jesus' message that failing to deal with the sin in the church has the power to cause even a huge, powerful church full of good works to crumble.

We look around and see or hear of churches splitting, dividing, and even closing—churches which perhaps were once bursting with life and miraculous works of the Holy Spirit. Perhaps this letter from Jesus to the church of Ephesus may explain why.

In Jesus' final word of encouragement to the Ephesian church, He commends them for the fact that they hate the evil works of the Nicolaitans, as *much as He does*. Let's briefly examine who these Nicolaitans were and what evil deeds they were doing.

The NIV Study Bible tells us:

> Nicolaitans: A heretical sect *within* the church that had worked out a compromise with the pagan society. They apparently taught that spiritual liberty gave them sufficient leeway to practice idolatry and immorality. Tradition identifies them with Nicolas, the proselyte from Antioch, who was one of the first seven deacons of the Jerusalem church (Acts 6:5), though the evidence is merely circumstantial. A similar group in the church at Pergamum held to the teaching of Balaam (Rev 2:14–15), and some at Thyatira were followers of the woman Jezebel (Rev 2:20). From their heretical tendencies it would appear that all three groups were Nicolaitans.[1]

We will come to the churches at Pergamum and Thyatira in chapters 6 and 7 respectively; but in Jesus' message to the church at Ephesus, He was saying that their hatred of the evil deeds of the Nicolaitans He held in their favor, because *He* hated these evil deeds as much as they did.

We must note that these people were *within* the larger church, not some small group of people set up as a "church" on their own. They were infiltrating and functioning *inside* the Christian church. We ought to take a serious note of this fact. What and whom exactly have *we* allowed to become settled and rooted in our churches without confronting and dealing with whatever sins they are bringing with them?

So, what evil deeds of the Nicolaitans did the believers in the church at Ephesus hate that Jesus also hated—that

He hated so much so that He would actively praise the Ephesians for their hatred? The Nicolaitans were Christian believers who were deceived into believing that spiritual liberty gave them leeway and freedom to compromise their Christian life by practicing the same things as the pagan society around them such as worshiping idols and engaging in immoral lifestyles.

In today's language, the *pagan society* is the world of unbelievers around us with the choices and lifestyles of those who do not know Jesus as their Lord and Savior, or those who have rejected Him. When we read what the Nicolaitans in the church at Ephesus were doing, doesn't this describe what we see happening in many churches today? People within the church are rising up and saying that their freedom in Christ gives them leeway to practice whatever form of immorality they choose or desire.

Idolatry is not only to be found in being overly fix-ated with our cars, homes, jobs, possessions, and money; but it can even been seen within the church. It is evident when we focus excessively on "high profile" preachers or worship bands, chasing them all around the country so that we can be at their next big conference or their next big gig. It is seen in craving the experience of it all rather than hungering and thirsting after God who gave those preachers or the worship bands their gifts that we have ended up worshiping instead.

Don't get me wrong, I am not knocking the preachers or the worship bands. They are doing what God has called them to do if their motives and their hearts are pure and right with Him. And I am not saying it is idolatry to go to these events. What I am hoping to point out is that if our time becomes consumed with this sort of activity at the expense of our personal "one-on-one" relationship with

God in the solitude of our "closet" at home, then I would suggest that excess attendance of even Christian events can develop into the sin of idolatry. We must worship the Creator not the preacher or the worship band that He has created.

There are many forms of idolatry and immorality lurking in the darkness of our Christian lives. If we would dig beneath the surface of the "holy" façade we put on and let the light of Christ shine into that darkness, I am sure that a multitude of evil deeds would scurry back into the darkness not wanting to be exposed to the light; rather like cockroaches beating a hasty retreat as soon as a light is switched on.

Concerning the proselyte Nicolas, the NIV Study Bible has told us that although the evidence is circumstantial, tradition has it that Nicolas was one of the first seven deacons in the Jerusalem church. Have we got that? This man was a *deacon, a leader* in the church; and he was teaching the believers that "anything goes," do whatever you like, it's all OK, God forgives you.

So there we have it. Within the church, which is the body of Christ, dwelt a group of believers originally initiated by a leader in the Jerusalem church who were practicing the evil deeds of Satan and thinking it was OK and that there would not be any consequences. These evil deeds were obviously practiced openly. They were not going on behind closed doors unnoticed because Jesus praises the rest of the church for hating these evil deeds (Rev. 2:6) and for not tolerating evil (v. 2). So it is clear that these were obvious and visible deeds of evil.

If Jesus hates these evil deeds that are visible, He must surely also hate the evil deeds of darkness that are not visible. These are the things that we do at home when no one is looking, the things that go on in our thoughts and our hearts, the things we watch and listen to, the magazines and books we read, the ungodly places we visit, or the ungodly conversations that we get drawn into and go along with.

This "spirit of the Nicolaitans" has not died. It is alive and rife in the church today. I would dare to suggest that not a single church exists today where the spirit of the Nicolaitans does not occupy a seat somewhere.

As the body of Christ, the church of Jesus Christ, are we just going to sit by and let this evil spirit be allowed to carry on deceiving believers into practicing its evil deeds within the church? As the church of Jesus Christ, we must *hate* these evil deeds as much as Jesus does. We must no longer tolerate them. We must expose them and confront them. We must challenge the believers who practice them to repent of their evil deeds and turn away from these things, to turn again to Jesus, to renounce every evil deed they are involved in and are still practicing, and to receive His cleansing and forgiveness.

To *renounce* something means to cut the activity off from our lives. We effectively draw a line in the sand and start again anew, having renounced our involvement in the hidden works of darkness, confessed them as sin, and repented of them.

Note that both Jesus and the other believers in the church at Ephesus hated the evil deeds of the Nicolaitans. They did not hate the people who practiced these things; they only hated the evil deeds. God loves His children and we are to love them too, but we are to hate the evil deeds and not tolerate them.

The Life Application Study Bible notes on page 2289 that in relation to Revelation 2:6:

We should accept and love all people and refuse to tolerate all evil. God cannot tolerate sin, and He expects us to stand against it. The world needs Christians who will stand for God's truth and point people towards right living.

Jesus is watching and still has these complaints against His churches. He expects us to take them seriously and is looking at us to take action.

Come on Church! Wake up!

Chapter 5

THE MESSAGE OF JESUS CHRIST
TO THE CHURCH IN SMYRNA

Write this letter to the angel of the church in Smyrna. This is the message from the one who is the First and the Last, who was dead but is now alive: I know about your suffering and your poverty—but you are rich! I know the blasphemy of those opposing you. They say they are Jews, but they are not, because their synagogue belongs to Satan. Don't be afraid of what you are about to suffer. The devil will throw some of you into prison to test you. You will suffer for ten days. But if you remain faithful even when facing death, I will give you the crown of life. Anyone with ears to hear must listen to the Spirit and understand what he is saying to the churches. Whoever is victorious will not be harmed by the second death.

—REVELATION 2:8–11

NOTICE IN THIS passage to the church in Smyrna that Jesus says that He knows they are suffering and they are facing poverty; *yet* He says that they are rich—not material richness but a spiritual richness that can only be received through the fires of affliction and poverty. Perhaps this would suggest that financial and material prosperity are not actually the right and entitlement of a believer. Yes, the Lord may bless us this way in order that we may help others with what He has blessed us with. But if we preach prosperity as the right and entitlement of every believer, we are off track from the Word of God. In this passage Jesus says that He knows their affliction and poverty, yet He doesn't appear to do anything to get them out of it. What He does do is encourage them by saying that despite their poverty, they are indeed rich. He knows that the wealth of their relationship with God is far more precious to them than financial and material wealth.

The church was being slandered by Jews who were so opposed to the Christians because they claimed that Jesus Christ was the Messiah. The Jews were waiting for the Messiah to come but did not believe that Jesus was Him, so they slandered the Christians. The Life Application Study Bible says in its notes on page 2290 that the Jews were serving Satan's purposes, not God's.

Jesus warned the church to expect suffering to the point of death. He encouraged them not to be afraid of what they may have to suffer but to remain faithful to their belief in Jesus, even to the very end. He would then personally give them the crown of life.

Jesus says that Satan may throw believers into prison for ten days. This may have been a real prison; but it may be any kind of "prison," such as a period of imprisonment of physical, emotional, mental, or spiritual affliction or distress, where we feel we are trapped and no end seems to be in sight.

As a church we need to hold on to the promises that Jesus gives to us concerning our future in the kingdom of heaven. Jesus gives glorious promises to faithful believers in the church who *continually overcome* everything that comes against them until He returns.

While Jesus doesn't mention any specific complaints He has against this church, I am sure we can be certain

tion for all mankind. It is already accomplished, but
has left the decision to *us* to choose whether or not
ill accept His free gift of eternal life through faith in
Christ.

ery unbeliever who dies unrepentant has chosen the
of his or her eternal destiny. That person *cannot*
e God. We are all responsible for the choices we
and for the resulting consequences of our choices.

owever, in this message to the church of Smyrna,
is speaking to *believers*. He is telling them that the
vers who overcome will not face the second death.
fore, is Jesus saying that *believers* who *don't* over-
—those who are still practicing evil deeds and
refuse to repent of them while still professing to be
vers and are occupying positions in the church—will
up having to face the second death—eternal torment
e lake of fire—and not end up in heaven like they
ght they would? Do the words of Jesus in the message
is church blast out of the water the concept/teaching
nce saved, always saved"?

od has taken me through a period of revelation and
y on this. As a result, it is now my personal belief that
lievers are somehow caught up in sin and *refuse to
nt of* it, and if they should suddenly die in that unre-
ant state having refused to heed God's warnings and
oving correction to return to Him, then those unre-
ant believers who choose to carry on sinning may find
iselves separated from God eternally in the lake of
longside all unbelievers.

sus warns of this time and time again throughout the
Testament. But I believe that Satan has deceived us
believing that hell is *only* a place for those who have
ccepted Jesus Christ as their Lord and Savior. Several

that they would have been faced with many t

fall into sin, and perhaps actually did. How

trast here is that since Jesus did *not* expres

against them, then it would suggest that th

been exposing, confronting, repenting, and

the sins within the church routinely and reg

of daily life. This would keep the church hea

as they took seriously Jesus' warnings throu

Testament to "be ready" for His second con

Oh, that this could be the case in today's

church at Smyrna should be held up as an e

Jesus requires of His church: one that end

poverty, slander, and suffering at the hand

gious" organizations; faces the threat of im

their faithful witness of Jesus Christ; and

God that He is in complete control of their

Jesus states that every *believer* who ove

be hurt by the second death. The first deat

death. The second death Jesus refers to is

that awaits all those whose names are no

Lamb's Book of Life (see Revelation 20:1–

it clear as to who will not enter the kin

when He says, "Nothing evil will be allov

anyone who practices shameful idolatry

but only those whose names are writte

Book of Life" (Rev. 21:27).

The lake of fire awaits all those who h

of their evil deeds and turned to Chr

Their destiny will be eternal torment in

the place of their destiny by their refus

Jesus can save them. God does not want

He wants all to come to repentance (2 F

is why Jesus died on the cross, to op

times Jesus says that many will call Him "Lord, Lord" but will not do the things He asks. He says that such people will not enter the kingdom of heaven, at other times He says they will be left outside the city gates, and at still other times He says they will cast into hell (Matt. 5:27–30; 7:13–14, 17–20; 13:24–30, 36–43; 18:8–9; Rev. 20:12–15; 21:7–9).

Jesus says:

> Not everyone who calls out to me, "Lord! Lord!" will enter the Kingdom of Heaven. Only those who actually do the will of my Father in heaven will enter. On judgment day many will say to me, "Lord! Lord! We prophesied in your name and cast out demons in your name and performed many miracles in your name." But I will reply, "I never knew you. Get away from me, you who break God's laws."
>
> —MATTHEW 7:21–23

The apostle Paul, speaking to the elders in the church at Ephesus, tells us:

> I declare today that I have been faithful. If anyone suffers eternal death, it is not my fault, for I didn't shrink from declaring all that God wants you to know.
>
> —ACTS 20:26–27

Dear readers, I encourage you and exhort you to study this serious matter for yourself, particularly if you are a Christian. All too often we become complacent, simply believing what we hear from the pulpit with the assumption that our preachers are teaching us correctly. But scriptures warn us that false teachers will rise up among us, leading people away into believing their false doctrine.

I cannot stress this strongly enough: *every* believer *must* take personal responsibility for their life in Christ to ensure that they are walking in the truth of God's Word and to be as sure as they can be about their eternal destiny. Every believer must study the Word of God for themselves and not just be fed secondhand through the pastor's teaching. After all, the pastor may have fallen into sin and been deceived into preaching half-truths and lies. He may be teaching a watered down version of the gospel, which may sound like the truth but in fact is a lie from Satan designed to lead all who believe it and follow it into the depths of hell.

If we are vigilant and diligent in daily reading and studying of the Word of God, when we are listening to a preacher who says something that is false doctrine, we will sense it deep in our spirit. When we hear a lie dressed up as a truth, our knowledge of the true Word of God will cut through the lie with the power of the double-edged sword. I have experienced this many times in my life. When I got home after such an incident, I have gone to the Word of God for confirmation that what I heard was a lie from Satan. God's Word has *never failed* to confirm it. Praise His wonderful name!

In view of this, wouldn't it be prudent for the members of the church and the church as a whole body to do everything they possibly can to keep examining their walk, their talk, their thoughts, their motives, and their actions to ensure that every aspect of their lives is meeting the requirements of God (see Revelation 3:2)? They need to ensure that they are continually living a repentant life and continually overcoming and living a life that is ready to meet the Lord at His second coming.

If we slack off from transparency and accountability within the church, we leave the doors wide open for Satan to creep in, to infiltrate the ranks, and to deceive us with the spirit of complacency and compromise. In a natural battle everyone is watching out for his fellow man and will pull him to safety if he is hit and wounded. Those who have been shot at by the enemy have their wounds tended to so that they can be restored back to some level of normality. Although, both in the natural and spiritual sense, once we have been hit by the enemy, our lives will always bear the scar of our encounter.

As a church, we must watch over our fellow brothers and sisters in Christ. We must be on the lookout for the works of Satan in the church and be courageous enough to approach those in the church whose lives are being lived in compromise and complacency concerning their faith in Christ. We must be courageous enough to help our brothers and sisters in Christ to pull the arrows of Satan out of their lives. We must demonstrate compassion toward them by helping them to dress their wounds by pouring in the healing balm of the truth of the Word of God and by leading them back to right living through obedience to His Word.

I believe this is the overcoming that Jesus is talking about. As a church we cannot stand by and watch our fellow believers get shot at by sin and then leave them to die a slow death at the hands of Satan and his demons, all because we are afraid of what sin we might discover if we went to help them. The church today seems to be so afraid of what it might discover if it lifts the lid on sin. Or it is afraid it won't know how to handle what it finds. So in the end the church decides to let sin remain undercover, in the dark, with the attitude of "what we don't know about won't hurt us." This mind-set is equivalent to signing your own death sentence; the consequence of this attitude is fatal for any member of the church who believes this lie from the pit of hell.

Come on Church! Wake up!

Chapter 6

THE MESSAGE OF JESUS CHRIST
TO THE CHURCH IN PERGAMUM

Write this letter to the angel of the church in Pergamum. This is the message from the one with the sharp two-edged sword: I know that you live in the city where Satan has his throne, yet you have remained loyal to me. You refused to deny me even when Antipas, my faithful witness, was martyred among you there in Satan's city. But I have a few complaints against you. You tolerate some among you whose teaching is like that of Balaam, who showed Balak how to trip up the people of Israel. He taught them to sin by eating food offered to idols and by committing sexual sin. In a similar way, you have some Nicolaitans among you who follow the same teaching. Repent of your sin, or I will come to you suddenly and fight against them with the sword of my mouth. Anyone with ears to hear must listen to the Spirit and understand what he is saying to the churches. To everyone who is victorious I will give some of the manna that has been hidden away in heaven. And I will give to each one a white stone, and on the stone will be engraved a new name that no one understands except the one who receives it.

—REVELATION 2:12–17

JESUS SAYS THAT His message is from "the one with the sharp two-edged sword." The "one" He is referring to is Himself, and His Word is the two-edged sword. As we know from scripture, His Word is powerful and mighty and is able to penetrate through to the deepest parts of us to convict us of sin and unrighteousness, to bring us to a place of godly sorrow which in turn will lead to us to repentance (see Hebrews 4:12).

Jesus is warning the church in Pergamum right from the beginning of His message that He is prepared to use His two-edged sword against them if they refuse to listen to His message and do what He requires. But first Jesus begins by praising the church for remaining loyal to Him while they have to live where they are, in the city where "Satan has his throne." For Jesus to call this city by such a name, it must have been an unbelievably demonic place where gross evil deeds were no doubt rife in the culture and environment. It must have been terrifying and unbearable for the Christians. Jesus praises them for remaining loyal to Him, even when Antipas, His faithful witness, was martyred among them in "Satan's city."

The Life Application Study Bible describes Pergamum in its notes on page 2290 as being the center of four cults and says that it rivaled Ephesus in its worship of idols. The chief god was Asclepius, and people from all over the world came to Pergamum to seek healing from this god. The other gods were Zeus, Dionysius, and Athene. Even the Roman Emperor was considered a god. Not much is known about Antipas, but it is clear that he was martyred for his faith in Jesus Christ. He obviously refused to compromise with the idolatrous and immoral pagan society around him. Even under this pressure, he remained faithful to Jesus unto death.

Even though Jesus praises them for their loyalty to Him under enormous pressure from the cults to compromise, He sees something wrong in the church and does not let it go unchallenged. He sees sin going on within the church and He confronts it.

In many of our modern-day churches, there is great emphasis on focusing on what is good and worthy of encouragement and praise, while ignoring glaringly obvious sinful practices. Evil will not go away by ignoring it. Jesus is showing us in all His letters to the churches how to "do church." We are to encourage and praise what is good, *and* we are to expose all evil and sinful practices and command those believers who practice them to repent and turn back to Christ.

So what is Jesus' complaint against this church?

> But I have a few complaints against you. You tolerate some among you whose teaching is like that of Balaam, who showed Balak how to trip up the people of Israel. He taught them to sin by eating foods offered to idols and by committing sexual sin. In a similar way, you have some Nicolaitans among you who follow the same teaching. Repent of your sin, or I will come to you suddenly and fight against them with the sword of my mouth.
> —REVELATION 2:14–16

So once again, Jesus is pointing out that there are people *within* the church who are tripping up God's children with false teaching, who are telling them that it is perfectly fine to eat foods that they know have been offered to idols and that it is fine to commit sexual sin.

Not only is there a group teaching this false doctrine but also, Jesus says, there is a group of Nicolaitans among them who are teaching the same things. So the believers in this church are exposing their ears to a double dose of evil teaching. Jesus is rebuking the *believers* for tolerating these false teachers. He tells them to repent of this sin and to turn away from the ways that they are tolerating this evil false teaching.

To *repent* means to turn away from something and do the total opposite of what you were doing. By calling them to repent, Jesus is telling these believers that they must no longer tolerate the behavior but must now do something about it; i.e., confront it and possibly remove those who are teaching it and practicing it if they refuse to repent.

There are times when church leaders need to and *must* take radical action to remove unrepentant sin from within the church. We know that Jesus will not tolerate evil remaining in the church, therefore, neither should we. Jesus warns the church that if they don't repent of their sin, He will personally come and fight against them with the sword of His mouth,—the two-edged sword of the Word of God.

Finally, Jesus finishes His message to the church with the promise of blessings in heaven to all those who are victorious and overcome. This would imply that Jesus is saying the opposite awaits believers who do not want to do the hard work of living victorious and overcoming lives. If they prefer to live complacent and compromising lives, more content to continue in the pleasures of this life than to repent of their ways and do whatever is necessary to make themselves and their lives ready for the return of the King of kings and Lord of lords, they are in great danger of not entering into the kingdom of heaven.

Come on Church! Wake up!

Chapter 7

THE MESSAGE OF JESUS CHRIST
TO THE CHURCH IN THYATIRA

Write this letter to the angel of the church in Thyatira. This is the message from the Son of God, whose eyes are like flames of fire, whose feet are like polished bronze: I know all the things you do. I have seen your love, your faith, your service, and your patient endurance. And I can see your constant improvement in all these things. But I have this complaint against you. You are permitting that woman—that Jezebel who calls herself a prophet—to lead my servants astray. She teaches them to commit sexual sin and to eat food offered to idols. I gave her time to repent, but she does not want to turn away from her immorality. Therefore, I will throw her on a bed of suffering, and those who commit adultery with her will suffer greatly unless they repent and turn away from her evil deeds. I will strike her children dead. Then all the churches will know that I am the one who searches out the thoughts and intentions of every person. And I will give to each of you whatever you deserve. But I also have a message for the rest of you in Thyatira who have not followed this false teaching ("deeper truths," as they call them—depths of Satan, actually). I will ask nothing more of you except that you hold tightly to what you have until I come. To all who are victorious, who obey me to the very end, To them I will give authority over all the nations. They will rule the nations with an iron rod and smash them like clay pots. They will have the same authority I received from my Father, and I will also give them the morning star! Anyone with ears to hear must listen to the Spirit and understand what he is saying to the churches.

*—*REVELATION 2:18–29

GAIN, JESUS STARTS His message to the church in Thyatira with words of praise and encouragement. He tells them that He knows all the things they do and that He has seen their love, their faith, their service, and their patient endurance. Not only that, He has seen their constant improvement in all these things.

It is so wonderful that Jesus notices these things and praises them for it. However, when we apply this to the church environment, this is where many churches stop. They major on praising and encouraging the flock for the good they are doing and the improvement they are making, which is great. *But* many suggest that it is not necessary to deal with sin in the church because it has all been taken care of on the cross—a phrase I have heard so many times in today's church. I have felt deep within me that such a mind-set is used as an excuse so that they don't have to do the painful and hard work of exposing, confronting, and dealing with persistent, repetitive, and habitual sin inside the church.

Such work is messy and dirty; but even Jesus got down on His knees and did the messy, dirty work of washing the disciples' feet. Surely this is the greatest example of having a "servant's heart" toward our fellow brothers and sisters in Christ. Jesus shows us what to do and then tells us to go and do likewise. His actions visibly instruct us to go and wash off the mess and the dirt from each other's lives (see John 13:1–17).

It would seem that no one wants to openly admit that there is sin inside the church in the lives of followers of Christ, let alone expose it and deal with it. The unspoken attitude toward it is that sinful practices will just go away on their own and that we mustn't focus on them as this gives glory to Satan. How far from biblical truth this attitude is! How it must grieve the heart of God when He sees His children making claims like this instead of seeking His Word for the truth about it. Scripture says that we must expose evil and deal with it according to God's Word, not pretend it doesn't exist or hope it will just disappear of its own accord.

Well, let's think about this a bit more seriously. Jesus came to earth as God in human flesh and dwelt among us (John 1:14). In His ministry He taught the disciples and all who followed Him how they should live their lives if they professed to be believers. He went to the cross, bore the full weight of the sins of the world in His body, and there He died. His work of the redemption of mankind was finished. His death had opened the way for every man, woman, and child from every race, tribe, and nation to receive eternal life. This was available *provided* they would repent of their ways and forsake their false gods, their false religions, and their false beliefs and put their faith, hope, and trust in Jesus Christ as their Lord and Savior.

After His burial He was raised to life by the almighty power of God and was seen by all of the disciples on many occasions who have testified and borne witness to His resurrection (Acts 1:1–3, KJV). After this Jesus ascended into heaven and is seated at the right hand of God (Eph. 1:20). *From* Jesus' ascended position, He is watching everything and sees and hears everything in the church on earth as He "walks among the seven gold lampstands" (Rev. 2:1).

Has it ever really occurred to us believers that Jesus is walking in and out of our churches, going from church to church to see and hear what is happening in them? So if our ascended Savior Jesus Christ, who sees sin of every sort still being allowed to dwell in the church unchecked, finds it necessary to confront the churches about it and command them to repent, how come *the church itself doesn't* think it is necessary?

This is the same Jesus who was crucified on the cross for our sins about whom we casually say, "Oh, we don't need to deal with sin because Jesus took care of it all on the cross." Let's remind ourselves of this one important fact: Jesus was crucified on the cross for the sins of the whole world, *yet after* He had left the earth and ascended into heaven, in the Book of Revelation He is still instructing believers in the church to repent of the sins they are still committing and turn back to Him. Well, from His ascended position after His crucifixion, either Jesus has got it wrong for still feeling it is necessary to confront the church about sins they are still allowing and practicing, *or we* have got it wrong by thinking we don't need to deal with sin inside the church.

I know without a shadow of doubt and as surely as God created me, that Jesus is *not* the one who is wrong. And so Jesus, who is *not* wrong and who is *not* a liar, from His ascended position in heaven proceeds to tell the church of His complaint against them. What He has to say to the church does not make for easy reading.

These are Jesus' words:

> But I have this complaint against you. You are permitting that woman—that Jezebel who calls herself a prophet—to lead my servants astray. She teaches them to commit sexual sin and to eat food offered to idols. I gave her time to repent, but she does not want to turn away from her immorality. Therefore, I will throw her on a bed of suffering and those who commit adultery with her will suffer greatly unless they repent and turn away from her evil deeds. I will strike her children

dead. Then all the churches will know that I am
the one who searches out the thoughts and intentions of every person. And I will give to each of
you whatever you deserve.

—REVELATION 2:20–23

Whoa! No wonder we don't hear this preached in the
church. I have been a Christian since 1992, and I cannot
recall having heard this preached anywhere. My guess is
that leaders are afraid to reveal this aspect of Jesus to the
believers because it does not fit into the description of the
"Jesus" that the modern church has sold to them for so
long. A watered-down version of Jesus has been preached
to unbelievers and believers alike in order to attract them,
win them, and keep them in the church.

If they dared to preach these hard-hitting truths of
Jesus, they are probably fearful that they would frighten
the flock away and lose everything they have spent years
building up with their watered-down doctrine. If the
church doesn't preach the *whole* truth, the half-truth that
they do preach will lead people into a false sense of secu-
rity. It leaves the doors wide open for Satan to come in and
deceive us through the preaching of half the truth.

Oh yes! Satan doesn't mind us only being taught the
nice half of the truths from God's Word. Satan is quite
happy for all believers to believe that they are going to
end up in heaven, regardless of what sins they allow themselves to get caught up in as believers. Satan is quite happy
for followers of Christ to remain blind to the truth that
they need to live continually repentant lives—every day,
every week, every month, every year—until Jesus returns.
To preach half the truth is to preach a lie. All lies are from

Satan, and all who love to live a lie will not be permitted entry into the kingdom of heaven (Rev. 22:15).

So Satan controls many preachers with a spirit of fear and deceives them into thinking that they do not need to preach this hard-hitting stuff. When my husband and I have found the courage to approach church leaders about preaching this type of scripture, we have both been witness to comments such as "we don't want to frighten people away from the church." But the passage above (Revelation 2:20–23) is the Word of Jesus to His churches. There must be serious stuff going on in the church for Him to write such a stern warning to them.

We need to realize that Jesus is speaking to *believers* in the church who are continuing to carry out sinful practices and evil deeds. This is *not* addressed to unbelievers. Jesus, who is full of grace and mercy, has even given these believers time to repent. But Jesus goes on to say that they don't want to repent or turn away from their immorality. Have we fully grasped this? The Son of God Himself loves these believers who are still sinning *so much* that He gives them time to repent and turn away from their sins, but they refuse to do so. (Let's not forget to include ourselves here.) They want to carry on practicing whatever vile, perverted, evil deed entices the desires of their flesh. They no doubt have a multitude of excuses and reasons why they are not going to repent, not even for the Son of God Himself—not even for Jesus, the one they claim to believe in.

And because they have rejected Jesus' extended time to repent and stubbornly refused to turn away from their sins, Jesus tells them of the consequences that they can now expect. What He says goes against every "doctrine" I have ever heard preached in the church. Obviously this doctrine I have heard must be the doctrine of man. Can you imagine many preachers standing up and saying what Jesus says in Revelation 2:22–23?

> Therefore, I will throw her on a bed of suffering, and those who commit adultery with her will greatly suffer, unless they repent and turn away from her evil deeds. I will strike her children dead.

These are Jesus' words to the church. Have you ever heard this preached? I haven't, not in twenty years of being a believer.

Let's break this message down into bite-sized pieces. In verse 22 it is referring to the woman Jezebel, known as a prophet in the church, who was teaching people *in* the church to do evil things, the same things as the Nicolaitans were doing (as we have previously seen in Jesus' letters to the churches at Ephesus and Pergamum). Because she refused to repent, yet still thinks it is OK to remain in the church, Jesus says He will throw her and all who practice what she teaches on a bed of suffering. Jesus doesn't say what this bed of suffering will be, but we could assume it would be any kind of suffering—physical, emotional, mental, relational, financial, spiritual, lack of provision, etc. It would seem from Jesus' words that *He* decides what the bed of suffering will be because He says, "I will throw her on a bed of suffering."

So from this scripture it is clear that we *can* and *will* experience suffering at the hand of God as a consequence of refusing to repent of the sins we are involved in as Christians. But let's get this straight; God doesn't want or desire for us to suffer. On the contrary, He loves us so much that He keeps giving us time to repent of the evil we are doing; He holds back on imposing the consequences; and He keeps warning us what *will* happen if we carry on ignoring Him. But in the end, if we willfully refuse to accept rebuke and correction from Him or from those He uses to warn and correct us, surely God is justified in bringing upon us what He has already warned us He will do.

Is what God says and does any different to the proper parenting skills we use in relationships with our own children? The right results are only achieved when boundaries and consequences are set and enforced when necessary. Relationships that are devoid of boundaries and consequences lead to a serious lack of respect for any form of authority, total selfishness, self-centeredness, and an attitude of "no one's gonna tell *me* what to do—not even God."

Jesus is saying in effect, "The choice is yours. I have warned you of the consequences of remaining unrepentant and I *will* carry out the consequences; but I am making *you* responsible as to whether or not I have to fulfill what I have warned you of."

The scripture says in the second part of verse 22, "And those who commit adultery with her will suffer greatly, unless they repent and turn away from her evil deeds." I think it needs to be mentioned that the term *adultery* is not just the literal term of sexual immorality. From a spiritual perspective it has a much wider meaning and encompasses anything that we are enticed into doing that is against God's holy Word in any way whatsoever. I would call it spiritual adultery or spiritual unfaithfulness, which means practicing *any* deeds that are contrary to God's Word. Anything that is against God's Word is evil; it is sin.

Following is a list of sinful behavior and evil practices that we could be involved in which affect our relationship with God and damage our witness for Jesus Christ. This list covers not only the *big* sins but also many subtle sins that we might ignore or make excuses for. We may often tolerate them but they are ungodly and we need to repent of them and change our behavior so that it is in accordance with the Word of God.

I have taken many of these sins from Jerry Bridges' book, *Respectable Sins*.[1]

LIST OF SINS

- **Murder**: Taking someone's life in any way (including your own life).

- **Theft**: Burglary, robbery, muggings, petty theft, shoplifting, taking things from your place of work for your own personal use without your employer's permission.

- **Sexual Sin**: Homosexuality, lesbianism, rape, sexual abuse, molestation, incest, adultery, fornication, lust, masturbation, pornography, pedophilia, any other form of sexual perversion.

- **Violence**: Any sort.

- **Fraud**: Any sort.

- **Coveting**: Desiring things that belong to other people.

- **Addictions/Obsessions**: Drugs, alcohol, smoking, sex, gambling.

- **Subtle Addictions**: Horoscopes; the following in excess: shopping, food, computer games, TV, mobile phone usage, Internet chat rooms, etc.

- **Anger**: Hatred, bitterness, resentment, strife, hostility, holding grudges, verbal outbursts, unforgiveness (any of these toward others, God, ourselves, or circumstances).

- **Control**: Includes manipulation, bullying, intimidation, domination, oppression, perfectionism.

- **Jealousy**: Including envy and competitiveness.

- **Fear and Worry**: Including anxiety, frustration, apprehension.

- **Discontentment**: About life, jobs, money, possessions, relationships, anything.

- **Pride**: Boasting, puffing ourselves up, superiority, self-righteousness, stubbornness, independence (the self-made man attitude), un-teachable attitude.

- **Vainglory**: Doing the right things with the wrong motive; i.e., doing good deeds because we want to be noticed and so that others will thank us and praise us.

- **Selfishness/Self-centeredness**: Demanding that our needs and wishes get met above everything else, selfish with our time and money, being inconsiderate and thoughtless of others, impatience, annoyance, irritability (toward others, ourselves, external situations beyond our control, and even toward God), self-pity.

- **Sins of the Tongue**: Gossip, foul language, harsh words, coarse joking, jesting (making fun of others), belittling and intimidating words, insults and slander, lying, deception, denial, pretence, bearing false witness, blasphemy/profanity, corrupting talk, sarcasm, unwarranted criticism, judgmentalism (assuming a situation and making a personal judgment about it based on inadequate/minimal information).

- **Unthankfulness**: Grumbling, complaining unnecessarily, moaning, lack of appreciation toward others, not showing or verbalizing our gratitude, "glass half empty" syndrome.

- **Lack of Self-Control**: Emotional outbursts that are uncontrolled; physical and verbal abuse; anger; overeating; excessive drinking; partying; overspending; acquiring possessions; excessive TV usage and program choice; computer usage and website choices; choice of books, magazines, and music; untidiness; secret lust and fantasy; other secret thoughts and imaginations.

- **Worldliness**: Lust for more (possessions, money, promotions, etc.); inappropriate dress to get ourselves noticed by others; inappropriate behavior to draw attention; going along with and following the practices of society around us and peer pressure in order to fit in and feel accepted and valued, even when we know that what we are succumbing to is unbiblical.

- **Ungodliness**: Living our life with no thought or regard for God whatsoever. Our lives display this through our words, our attitudes, and our actions.

- **Idolatry**: Putting anything else over and above God and focusing on it or pursuing it obsessively; e.g., sports, sports stars, celebrities, soap operas and other TV programs, reality TV, cars, possessions, money, homes, jobs, the latest gadgets, our looks, and even idolizing our spouse or our children.

- **Other Attitudes/Feelings/Emotions**: Indifference, aloofness, cynicism, callousness, coldness, hard-heartedness.

- **Other Spiritual Experiences**: Witchcraft; Satanism; the occult; New Age and other alternative spiritualism; consulting mediums, clairvoyants, etc.; dowsing; crystals; orbs; Ouija Boards; other "séance" activities; alternative healing where faith in God/Jesus is absent; contacting the spirits of the dead; ghost-hunting; hypnosis and hypnotherapy or anything involving mind control; divining; Eastern mystic spiritualism; any faith or religion that denies God *and* His Son Jesus Christ as the Messiah and our Lord and Savior; worship and obsession of angels; Freemasonry and other associated/affiliated organizations; palm reading; fortune telling; tarot cards; tea-leaf reading; horoscopes; astrology; yoga; levitation; channeling; scientology; any cults even so-called Christian cults.

This list is extensive but not exhaustive. I am sure there are other sins that I have overlooked which you could add to the list above.

So if anyone in the church is enticing us through false teaching to do anything that is not in keeping with the Word of God, we must refuse to listen to it and refuse to accept it. We must then expose those who are messengers of Satan masquerading as angels of light (2 Cor. 11:14–15). Jesus warns us that if we get caught up in their false teaching and begin to follow and practice what they say, we too will end up suffering greatly, *unless* we repent and turn away from the evil deeds we are being enticed and deceived into practicing.

Wow! Jesus does it again! He gives time to repent to those who get caught up in these webs of sin. Jesus *endlessly* gives opportunities for believers to repent and turn away from their evil deeds. His love, grace, and mercy toward us will continue until our dying breath. But as believers we absolutely must make sure that we have repented of whatever we have allowed ourselves to get caught up in *before* we die. If we are still wallowing around in our life of sin at the moment of our death, there is no more opportunity to repent. It needs to be done while we are still alive on earth. There are eternal consequences if we die as an unrepentant believer.

Jesus has left the choice with us. And if our choice is to refuse His gracious and loving rebuke and correction, we leave Him no other choice than to bring into being the consequences He has warned us of.

In verse 23 Jesus says, "I will strike her children dead." I will not profess to know whether Jesus meant this literally or in some other manner. But I do know the "her" He is referring to is the false prophet Jezebel who is teaching and leading the people of God, the Christians, to commit evil deeds. So this would be a reference to *all* false prophets and false teachers in all Christian churches throughout history, including the church today. The use of the words *her children* could mean the literal offspring of each false prophet or it could mean the followers of the false prophets. Either way, what Jesus says will happen to them is catastrophic; and I am not sure that I possess enough wisdom to make much comment.

From my limited knowledge, all I know is the evidence I see and hear about the "death sentence" that hangs over the lives of those caught up in homosexuality and other sexual perversions and drug, alcohol, and smoking addictions. Evidence has shown that children born to those addicted to drugs, alcohol, and smoking are often born already addicted to these substances or have serious health complications at birth due to the lifestyles of the parents. Many babies and children die because they have inherited their parent's addiction. Parents who have HIV/AIDS which they may have contracted due to a lifestyle of sexual immorality often pass this "death sentence" on to their unborn children in the womb; and these babies are born with a deadly disease through no fault of their own.

The choices the parents make regarding their lifestyles can be passed on to the children. Parents who smoke in the presence of their children cause them to inhale nicotine, increasing their likelihood of developing lung cancer, which can lead to a premature death for these children. Any lifestyle choice for a Christian that is contrary to God's holy Word has the potential to impact the life of their children. Children learn by following an example, whether good or bad. Children often follow the ungodly practices of their parents, believing that it is OK to do them. This action will lead them into spiritual death and an eternity in hell if it is not repented of.

Jesus warns us to repent and turn away from all forms of immorality; but if we still refuse to do so, then the consequences *will* follow, and we *cannot* blame God. God constantly gives us the choice and the chance to change the course of our lives, the lives of our children, and the lives of their children throughout all generations. He loves us unrelentingly and unendingly. There is never a moment that goes by where He doesn't give us the opportunity to repent from whatever ungodliness we have fallen into. In fact, with every breath that we take, there is another opportunity to repent. With every beat of our heart, God gives us another chance to repent. While we are still alive on this earth, He doesn't just give us one opportunity and then say, "Sorry, that's your lot."

But there will be *no* more chances to repent *after* we have died, only judgment. This is why it is absolutely vital that we live repentant lives before God with reverential fear of His holy, righteous, and just nature. If we are disobedient, rebellious, sinful, and unrepentant at the time we die, we will not escape God's judgment for the way we have lived our lives any less than total unbelievers just because we are Christians. Ephesians 5:6–7 tells us, "Don't be fooled by those who try to excuse these sins, for the anger of God will fall on all who disobey Him. Don't participate in the things these people do."

We cannot possibly profess to be believers if our lives are no different than the lives and lifestyles of unbelievers. Wherever we are and whatever circumstances we are in, no matter how many times we may have ended up falling into sinful ways, God says, "Repent and turn from [your] evil deeds" (Rev. 2:22).

But ultimately we must come to a point in our life in Christ where we are so full of disgust and regret at what we have deliberately refused to repent of that it causes us to be broken. We become filled with shame and sorrow that we could have been so deceived by those whom Satan uses on this earth to entice us into practicing evil deeds that are like spit and vomit in the face of our Savior Jesus Christ. It should cause us to want to turn away from our evil deeds forever and to remain alert and vigilant in our daily walk in Christ, super-sensitive to every possibility where Satan and his demons would attempt to ensnare us again.

We must change our attitude toward sin. Every time sin tries to deceive us, entice us, or ensnare us, we must view these onslaughts of the evil one as opportunities to overcome the sin and grow spiritually rather than something that is going to defeat us and cause us to fall again. Satan wants us to believe we will *never* overcome the sins we have become caught up in. He wants us to believe that we are permanently trapped in our evil deeds and that we will never escape from them. He attempts to sear this mind-set into the core of our being; yet this is all a lie from the father of lies himself, Satan.

The truth is that Jesus sees us wallowing in our sins and He keeps throwing us a lifeline. That lifeline is called *repentance*. It is actually an incredibly humbling gift that God wants us to grab hold of. In Acts 11:18b, Paul refers to it as "the privilege of repenting." Once we have got a hold of what it means for a believer to continually live a repentant lifestyle and to actively put this into practice on a moment by moment basis, we truly can have the confidence of entering the gates of heaven. Each time we repent and turn away from our evil deeds and overcome them, our relationship with God is restored.

When we choose to remain in the grip of our evil deeds, it is *our* choice that fractures our relationship with God. We are fully responsible for every break in our relationship with Him. He shows us what is wrong, instructs us what to do to put it right, and then leaves it up to us.

In the final part of Revelation 2:23, Jesus goes on to say that when these awful consequences become manifest, "All the churches will know that I am the one who searches out the thoughts and intentions of every person. And I will give to each of you whatever you deserve." Hebrews 4:13 confirms this: "Nothing in all creation is hidden from God. Everything is naked and exposed before his eyes, and he is the one to whom we are accountable."

So, Jesus is saying that He can see into the minds, hearts, and souls of everyone. Remember, He is addressing this to *believers* and He sees every motive and thought and intention inside us, whether it is for good or evil. Therefore, every one of our thoughts, motives, and intentions and every word and action that is ungodly and evil which we refuse to repent of, we will be held to account for by the Lord; and we will receive what we deserve.

We must live our lives in Christ with pure, right, just, and honorable motives toward each other, seeking to do God's will in every area of our lives, *every day*—not just with the appearance of godliness on a Sunday morning and mid-week house group meeting. If five days a week we are living our lives in sinful, evil ways with barely any thought about God, then our lives in Christ are a lie, a sham, and hypocrisy. That revelation should not make us give up but should ignite the fire of the Holy Spirit in us to repent and clean out the temple.

Now that we have studied Jesus' complaint against the church and the consequences that are awaiting those who refuse to repent, let us continue with the rest of Jesus' message to the church.

In Revelation 2:24–25, Jesus addresses the rest of the church in Thyatira:

> But I also have a message for the rest of you in Thyatira *who have not followed this false teaching* ("deeper truths," as they call them—depths of Satan, actually). I will ask nothing more of you, except that you hold tightly to what you have until I come (emphasis added).

I absolutely love these verses! The description of this false teaching is absolutely spot-on and cuts through the veneer of what so many alternative spiritual organizations and religions of today call deeper truths. Jesus is saying with the power of the words of His double-edged sword that these false teachings are not deeper truths, as these false teachers and their organizations would have you believe. Jesus knows exactly what they are: He says they are "depths of Satan, actually." Whoa! When I read this it makes me want to jump up and down and shout praises to God with every fiber of my being.

Jesus exposes all false teaching for what it is. Every spiritual teaching that is contrary to the holy Word of God comes from the depths where Satan has his throne—in the pit of hell. Yet we allow ourselves to be so easily deceived by him and his agents here on earth. Why? Because we do not weigh and measure what we hear from these false teachers against the truth of God's Word

We just hear their teachings and think, *Oh, that sounds good, that sounds like the sort of thing I want to hear and want to do.* And so we have taken Satan's bait and are slowly reeled into his net of deception. We are not really aware of it until we are well and truly tangled up in it. Satan's lies and deceptions are so juicy and nice that we don't realize his bait is laced with enough poison to destroy us.

The term *deeper truths* sounds really nice and spiritual doesn't it? If these deeper truths were advertised on an alternative spiritual billboard or leaflet as "depths of Satan," most people (including believers) wouldn't go anywhere near them. So the truth, God's truth, is that these deeper truths are actually lies, Satan's lies, dressed up to look and sound like really lovely, liberating truths. But the truth is they are designed to ensnare and destroy us.

Then Jesus says something to the believers who are *not* following these false teachings. The words He speaks are like a soothing balm being poured continually into a dry, thirsty, and weary soul. His words should be enough to cause us all to cast off the relentless evil spirit that cracks its whip at us, pressuring us to do endless, wearying works that drain us emotionally, physically, mentally, and spiritually until we are burned out.

What are these beautiful, loving, gracious, and soothing words that Jesus speaks to those believers who have *not* followed false teaching? "I will ask nothing more of you, except that you hold tightly to what you have until I come" (Rev. 2:24–25).

Jesus knows that we live in this world and have to work and run our homes, cars, family, shopping, etc. But in the midst of our lives on earth, His words say to me, "Stop! Stop striving, stop doing, stop craving, and stop clamoring. Your life is more than all of this. Stop, rest, seek Me, and find Me amidst all the activity that makes up your life on earth. At least half of what you feel you have to do is not even necessary; you just think it is. So you fill up your life with it because you want to be achieving something all the time at the expense of the peace and the rest I want to give you. I am waiting for you to stop so that I can give you what you really need. This surpasses all that you think you want."

Jesus is giving us permission to do nothing more than to hold tightly to what we have until He comes. What does this mean? I am certain He doesn't mean we can just sit around doing nothing; and He certainly doesn't mean for us to hold tightly to our possessions and our money. What He means is for us to hold tightly to our faith in Him and the truth of His Word. He means to live our lives in accordance with His Word, to not become indifferent or complacent about our faith, and to not compromise our lives and our faith by tolerating false doctrines and evil deeds. He means living our lives in Christ daily with repentant hearts, in reverential fear of the Lord, and with the knowledge that He *is* coming back and that it will happen suddenly without notice and when we least expect it.

Jesus wants to find us "ready" when He returns. The major part of "being ready" is what needs to take place inside us. Doing all the good works in the whole world will not make us clean and pure inside. I would dare to suggest that a great many people are overly active and busy in the church because they are afraid to stop and deal with what they know is inside them. So they join as many activities and committees as they possibly can so that they never have to stop and face the ugliness of the sin inside them.

But Jesus' Word pursues us relentlessly because He wants us to face these things that we run and hide from. He wants us to repent and turn away from them and overcome them and be victorious over them. His blessings are already stored up in heaven for those who do this.

Come on Church! Wake Up!

Chapter 8

THE MESSAGE OF JESUS CHRIST TO THE CHURCH IN SARDIS

Write this letter to the angel of the church in Sardis. This is the message from the one who has the sevenfold Spirit of God and the seven stars: I know all the things you do, and that you have a reputation for being alive—but you are dead. Wake up! Strengthen what little remains, for even what is left is almost dead. I find that your actions do not meet the requirements of my God. Go back to what you heard and believed at first; hold to it firmly. Repent and turn to me again. If you don't wake up, I will come to you suddenly, as unexpected as a thief. Yet there are some in the church in Sardis who have not soiled their clothes with evil. They will walk with me in white, for they are worthy. All who are victorious will be clothed in white. I will never erase their names from the Book of Life, but I will announce before my Father and his angels that they are mine. Anyone with ears to hear must listen to the Spirit and understand what he is saying to the churches.

—REVELATION 3:1–6

JESUS STARTS IMMEDIATELY with His complaint against this church in Sardis. To all intents and purposes they look like they are fully alive to those around them. They have a reputation for being "alive," so they look like they have got it all together, no doubt operating in the spiritual gifts, etc. But Jesus says, "You are dead." He sees beyond the outward appearance that is created to impress man and can see what is being neglected within.

He tells them, "Wake up! Strengthen what little remains, for even what is left is almost dead" (v. 2). Whatever it is they are neglecting, if they don't wake up and shake themselves out of their spiritual slumber, their neglect has the potential to cause the church to die.

Jesus then says some words that ought to cause every believer on earth to stop in their tracks on a daily basis and examine their lives in Christ. Here are Jesus' words: *"I find that your actions do not meet the requirements of My God"* (v. 2, emphasis added). Such words from our Savior ought to cause us to fall flat on our faces in repentance and in reverential fear of the Lord.

Jesus then tells them what they need to do to wake up and come back to life. He tells them, "Go back to what you *heard* and *believed at first*; hold to it firmly. Repent and turn to me again. If you don't wake up I will come to you suddenly, as unexpected as a thief" (v. 3, emphasis added).

The church appears to have gone off on tangents from what they first heard and believed. Possibly they got sidetracked into the latest spiritual thing, or perhaps they were focusing and majoring on "experiences" rather than on God Himself. In the process, they appear to have forgotten what they first heard and believed and may have ended up neglecting to preach it at all. They may have been focusing on specific types of meetings and services, such as healing and deliverance and other gifts, but failed to preach the gospel, which would expose sin and call people to repentance.

I am merely speculating here, but am attempting to examine what could be happening in a church when it has forgotten what it first heard and believed. To me it would mean that a multitude of other things and experiences have crept in and taken over, such as endless activity, outreaches, camps, or worship events, etc. These in themselves are good, but if majored on they have the potential to cause the church to neglect what it first heard and believed.

Jesus is telling them to stop all this activity that has given them a reputation that makes them look "alive." All that this achieves is the satisfaction of impressing others in the wider Christian circle. A church may end up with a big name for itself, and many then flock to it. But we hear of many such churches that end up being sacrificed on the altar of neglect. If our outward activity and reputation as a church does not allow the Holy Spirit to bring about conviction of sin and lead people to repentance, then our activity and reputation is worthless in God's eyes.

Jesus tells the church to stop what they are doing and to start doing what they first heard and believed and to hold to it firmly. He also tells them to repent of what they have allowed themselves to get caught up in and to turn back to Him again. He warns the church that if they don't wake up, He will come to them suddenly, as unexpected as a thief. What does a thief do? A thief takes away our most precious and valuable possessions while we are unaware of it. It is only after the thief has been and gone that we suddenly discover our great loss.

It would seem from Jesus' message to the church that if the church doesn't wake up and listen to His warning and do what He says, He will come and remove "what little remains" (v. 2) and then the church will be truly dead— another lampstand snuffed out.

True to His nature of grace and love, Jesus ends His

message to the church with the most amazing promise to those "who have not soiled their clothes with evil" (v. 4).

Here are Jesus' words in verses 4 and 5:

> Yet there are some in the church in Sardis who have not soiled their clothes with evil. They will walk with me in white, for they are worthy. *All who are victorious will be clothed in white. I will never erase their names from the Book of Life, but I will announce before my Father and His angels that they are mine* (emphasis added).

I almost cannot contain myself when I read Jesus' precious words of promise to "all who are victorious." Tears of joy and thankfulness of heart overwhelm me.

These words of Jesus ought to spur us on to overcome every form of evil that seeks to devour us. We must never forget what Jesus promises to all who overcome. We must hold these promises in front of our eyes and sear them in our minds and our hearts. Then when evil comes knocking at our door (and I can assure you that it will, continually until the day of Jesus' return), the promises that Jesus has spoken to us in His Word will flash into our minds to remind us of all the glorious things that await those who are victorious and overcome to the very end.

Come on Church! Wake up!

Chapter 9

THE MESSAGE OF JESUS CHRIST TO THE CHURCH IN PHILADELPHIA

Write this letter to the angel of the church in Philadelphia. This is the message from the one who is holy and true, the one who has the key of David. What he opens, no one can close; and what he closes, no one can open: I know all the things you do, and I have opened a door for you that no one can close. You have little strength, yet you obeyed my word and did not deny me. Look, I will force those who belong to Satan's synagogue—those liars who say they are Jews but are not—to come and bow down at your feet. They will acknowledge that you are the ones I love. Because you have obeyed my command to persevere, I will protect you from the great time of testing that will come upon the whole world to test those who belong to this world. I am coming soon. Hold on to what you have, so that no one will take away your crown. All who are victorious will become pillars in the Temple of my God, and they will never have to leave it. And I will write on them the name of my God, and they will be citizens in the city of my God—the new Jerusalem that comes down from heaven from my God. And I will also write on them my new name. Anyone with ears to hear must listen to the Spirit and understand what he is saying to the churches.

—REVELATION 3:7–13

JESUS DOESN'T HAVE any complaint against the church at Philadelphia. Instead He sees the things they do and He is opening doors for them that He says no man can close. He encourages them for obeying His Word and for not denying Him, even though they have little strength. This should encourage all of us who feel weary in the intense battle that is raging in the heavenly realms as the last days escalate. Jesus actually sees how little strength we have left and encourages us for still remaining obedient to Him and for not denying Him, no matter how weary we feel.

He says that He will force those who belong to Satan's synagogue to come and bow at the feet of the believers and to acknowledge that they (the believers) are the ones that Jesus loves. Let us remind ourselves from Jesus' message to the church in Smyrna that those who belong to Satan's synagogue are involved in false religions and worship gods and idols other than the one true God, the Father of our Lord and Savior Jesus Christ. Those false religions are "spiritual" organizations that teach false doctrine and lead people to put their faith in anything other than Jesus Christ.

Some religious organizations are so deceitful that they will even use the name of Jesus Christ in their doctrines and principles but do not actually preach the gospel. They will claim that there are many ways to believe in Jesus and that whatever way suits you will still get you in to heaven when you die. So many people are falling into this trap as the End Times close in.

Because this church has obeyed Jesus' command to persevere, He comforts them by telling them that He will protect them from the great time of testing that will come upon the whole world to test those who belong to this world; i.e., those who have rejected Jesus or who refuse to believe in Him. Such people actually belong to Satan, whether they realize it or not. If we are obeying and overcoming in our daily lives in Christ, Jesus will protect us when the great time of testing comes upon the world. We will not be affected by it. Praise to the Lord!

He exhorts them to hold on to what they have (spiritually speaking) so that no one will take away their crown, which is the crown of life Jesus mentioned to the church in Smyrna (Rev. 2:10). Once again Jesus promises the church blessings that await those who are victorious. They will become pillars in the temple of God. Pillars are designed with such strength that they are able to hold huge buildings in place. Imagine God giving the people in the church who have little strength (v. 8) here on earth such incredible strength when they get to heaven that they will eternally be pillars in the temple of God. Wow!

He also says that we will never have to leave the temple of God, and that Jesus Himself will write the name of God on us. And He will also write on us a new name that He alone will give us. Many of us throughout life have suffered the devastating effects of being called horrible names or labeled as idiots, failures, hopeless, useless, good for nothing, etc. What amazing comfort to know that all that we suffer and endure victoriously on earth will be reversed in heaven by Jesus, and He will give us each a new name. For certain, the new name He gives us will completely erase the painful memories of the evil names that have been spoken into our lives by those we trusted to love us.

Isn't Jesus wonderful?

Chapter 10

THE MESSAGE OF JESUS CHRIST
TO THE CHURCH IN LAODICEA

Write this letter to the angel of the church in Laodicea. This is the message from the one who is the Amen—the faithful and true witness, the beginning of God's new creation: I know all the things you do, that you are neither hot nor cold. I wish that you were one or the other! But since you are like lukewarm water, neither hot nor cold, I will spit you out of my mouth! You say, "I am rich. I have everything I want. I don't need a thing!" And you don't realize that you are wretched and miserable and poor and blind and naked. So I advise you to buy gold from me—gold that has been purified by fire. Then you will be rich. Also buy white garments from me so you will not be shamed by your nakedness, and ointment for your eyes so you will be able to see. I correct and discipline everyone I love. So be diligent and turn from your indifference. Look! I stand at the door and knock. If you hear my voice and open the door, I will come in, and we will share a meal together as friends. Those who are victorious will sit with me on my throne, just as I was victorious and sat with my Father on his throne. Anyone with ears to hear must listen to the Spirit and understand what he is saying to the churches.

—REVELATION 3:14–22

WHAT A CONTRAST this message to the church in Laodicea is when compared with Jesus' message to the church in Philadelphia. He has no words of encouragement to give them. He describes everything they do as lukewarm. What they are doing, we can assume, is a half-hearted attempt—"going through the motions" or possibly "having the appearance of godliness but denying the power thereof" (2 Tim. 3:5, KJV). Jesus detests this pretence so much that He says He will spit them out of His mouth.

The church boasts that it is rich; it has everything it wants and doesn't need a thing. This is obviously a visibly prosperous church, no doubt with very wealthy and prosperous members. Yet Jesus tells the members that with all the boasting of their prosperity, they don't realize that they are in fact wretched, miserable, poor, blind, and naked.

They have trusted in their worldly wealth to meet their needs and that has blinded them to the truth and reality that it is their relationship with God through Jesus Christ that is meant to make them rich—spiritually rich. They have forgotten this and are instead boasting about their material richness.

Jesus tells them in verse 18 that it is from Him that they must get gold that has been purified by fire, white garments to cover their "nakedness," and ointment for their eyes so that they can see clearly. What Jesus is saying to us is that He *will* expose us to our sin of "Hey, look at us! Aren't we wonderful and blessed, we are so prosperous! We have got it all together; we've got fine clothes and much wealth and God has given us a vision of prosperity." He will then show us that spiritually speaking we are the total opposite of what our outward appearance is and that we have been blinded by the sin of our boasting in what we materially possess.

Jesus says that He corrects those He loves. So even though we fall into sin again and again as believers, He still loves us and with His words of correction He shows us what is wrong and tells us how to put it right. He tells us to turn from our indifference and to be diligent.

He says He is standing outside the door knocking. He wants us to hear His voice and open the door and let Him come in so that He can have a relationship with us as friends. It is our indifference to Him that is preventing us from hearing Him knocking or hearing His voice. Our indifference causes us to get caught up in everything else except our relationship with Him.

But His promise to believers who are victorious is that they will sit with Him on His throne in the same way that He was victorious (over sin and death on the cross) and now sits with His Father on His throne.

EPILOGUE

THIS IS THE end of the messages of Jesus Christ to His churches. So what have we learned? Have we had ears to hear and listened to the Spirit and understood what He is saying to the churches? While I have been writing this book, I have shed many tears for what may come upon many churches and their individual members if they continue the way they are—if they refuse to listen to what Jesus is saying and refuse to live continually repentant lives.

You will recall that I started writing this book two days after being afflicted with a sudden, strange illness that seemed to hit me out of nowhere. I noticed, while writing about the church in Smyrna, that Jesus said, "Don't be afraid of what you are about to suffer. The devil will throw some of you into prison to test you. You will suffer for ten days" (Rev. 2:10).

During the illness I felt extremely weak and weary and in pain and was not able to leave the house. The illness seemed to engulf me, and I could not do even simple things. I felt like I had been locked in a "prison," unable to escape from it because of the suffering I had to endure. On one particular day I became aware that my body was beginning to return to its normal function. I counted up the number of days that I had been in this "prison" of suffering—it was ten days. On the eleventh day I noticed the first improvements in my body. Such realization was a meaningful and sacred moment for me; a moment that makes me really understand the love, the majesty, the faithfulness, and the holiness of God.

He is so loving, yet so holy, that every single thing that I have read from His Word and all that He has revealed to me in the writing of this book makes me tremble in the depths of my being with reverential fear of His truth and His justice. The truth is that God's love for all who profess to believe in Him will not permit Him to turn a blind eye at repeated sin within His church. This is true no matter what we think or what false doctrine we have heard and believed that we allow to "comfort" us with its deception.

It is time for the global church of Jesus Christ and all its members to grasp hold of the revelation that our Lord and Savior Jesus Christ is watching. From His ascended position in heaven at the right hand of His Father, the Lord God Almighty, He sees every move that we make and every deed that we do. He knows every motive and intent of our heart and every thought in our mind, and He hears every word that we say. And because of this, He is speaking through His messages to the churches in the Book of Revelation to the church today and to every church until He returns.

What Jesus says *is* the truth. Everything and anything that is contrary to His truth is a lie of Satan designed to steal, kill, and destroy what we have in Christ (John 10:10) and what we believe about Christ and eternity. As believers, we need to stop being persuaded and tossed about by every wind of doctrine that blows our way (Eph. 4:14) and get back to what we have heard and believed at first and hold firmly to it. We need to resist every form of evil that tries to deceive us and steal the truth from us and lead us astray into all sorts of wickedness and evil practices.

Having gone through this "prison" of suffering for a period of ten days in order to write the initial draft of this book, as a fellow sister in Christ and a servant of the Lord

Jesus Christ, I exhort you, individually and as a global Church, to take this message of Jesus extremely seriously. As we read the messages that Jesus has written to the churches, we see that the consequences that will come to bear in the lives of those within the church who remain unrepentant are enormous. Jesus is *not* joking—yet we treat His messages as if He is.

The time is short; each day is a day nearer to His return. It will come suddenly, when we least expect it. No one knows the hour or the day of His return, not the angels, not even Jesus Himself, but only the Father (Mark 13:32; Matt. 24:36). We do not want to be found naked and ashamed at His return (Rev. 16:15).

Let us all, with all humility, fall on our faces before God, crushed by the weight of the sins we have allowed to so easily deceive and ensnare us. Let the weight of our shame be turned into engulfing godly sorrow that leads us to repentance. As we confess our sins to God on a daily or even hourly basis, "He is faithful and just to forgive us our sins and to cleanse us from all unrighteousness" (1 John 1:9, NKJV).

Jesus is at the right hand of His Father waiting to receive His pure, spotless bride. Every earthly bride takes a great deal of time and hard work to prepare herself for her wedding so that when her groom sees her walking toward him, he is captivated by the gloriousness of her beauty. God requires that the bride (all of us who are believers) for His Son is pure and spotless, holy, and without fault (Eph. 5:27).

In effect, Jesus' messages to the churches are saying that your continual sins are soiling your wedding garment. Repent of your sins, turn again to Jesus, and do as He requires so that your garment is cleansed. Otherwise He cannot receive you as His bride.

The time is coming when the last trump shall sound,

when the Lord will return and we will all stand before the judgment seat of Christ. Jesus is pleading for us to make ourselves ready for His return and is warning us of the *real* consequences that await any believer who is living a life contrary to His Word.

Are *you* ready?

Are *we* ready?

The time is short—it may be very short. Let us wake up *now* and examine ourselves. Let's rid our minds, our hearts, our souls, our bodies, and our lives of *everything* that is not in keeping with the requirements of God, *everything* that would disqualify us from receiving what He has promised to those who love Him *and* obey His Word and His commands.

We have been created *by* God, for *His* purposes, for *His* glory. Let us live our lives with purity of heart, mind, soul, and body. Let us confess and repent of our sins *as they occur*, so that our garment is continually being cleansed from all unrighteousness by the precious blood of Christ.

A glorious eternal future awaits those who believe and are living their lives on earth in continual readiness for the sound of "the last trump" (1 Cor. 15:52, KJV). It is time to wake up out of our complacent and compromising slumber. If, in these last days, we still choose not to wake up, we cannot make the excuse that we were not warned of the consequences.

As a sister-in-Christ to all who believe, I will make my final heartfelt plea to *every* reader who holds this book in their hands and has made it through to this final page: please *wake up!* Because a time *will* come when it will be too late.

Appendix A

WORDS FROM OSWALD CHAMBERS

If a person cannot go to God, it is because he has something secret which he does not intend to give up—he may admit his sin, but would no more give up that thing than he could fly under his own power. It is impossible to deal sympathetically with people like that. We must reach deep down in their lives to the root of the problem, which will cause hostility and resentment towards the message. People want the blessing of God, but they can't stand something that pierces right through to the heart of the matter.

If you are sensitive to God's way, your message as His servant will be merciless and insistent, cutting to the very root. Otherwise, there will be no healing. We must drive the message home so forcefully that a person cannot possibly hide, but must apply its truth. Deal with people where they are, until they begin to realize their true need. Then hold high the standard of Jesus for their lives.[1]

The calling of a New Testament worker is to expose sin and to reveal Jesus Christ as Savior. Consequently he [the worker] cannot always be charming and friendly, but must be willing to be stern to accomplish major surgery. We are sent

by God to lift up Jesus Christ, not to give wonderful beautiful speeches. We must be willing to
examine others as deeply as God has examined us.
We must also be sharply intent on sensing those
scripture passages that will drive the truth home,
and then not be afraid to apply them.[2]

Appendix B

THE SWORD OF THE SPIRIT

Do not bring any detestable objects into your home, for then you will be destroyed, just like them. You must utterly detest such things, for they are set apart for destruction.

—Deuteronomy 7:26

Wash yourselves and be clean! Get your sins out of my sight. Give up your evil ways.

—Isaiah 1:16

But when he saw many Pharisees and Sadducees coming to watch him baptize, he denounced them. "You brood of snakes!" he exclaimed. "Who warned you to flee God's coming wrath? Prove by the way you live that you have repented of your sins and turned to God. Don't just say to each other, 'We're safe, for we are descendants of Abraham.' That means nothing, for I tell you, God can create children of Abraham from these very stones. Even now the axe of God's judgment is poised, ready to sever the roots of the trees. Yes, every tree that does not produce good fruit will be chopped down and thrown into the fire."

—Matthew 3:7–10

He is ready to separate the chaff from the wheat with his winnowing fork. Then he will clean up the threshing area, gathering the wheat into his barn but burning the chaff with never-ending fire.

—MATTHEW 3:12

So if your eye—even your good eye—causes you to lust, gouge it out and throw it away. It is better for you to lose one part of your body than for your whole body to be thrown into hell. And if your hand—even your stronger hand—causes you to sin, cut it off and throw it away. It is better for you to lose one part of your body than for your whole body to be thrown into hell.

—MATTHEW 5:29–30

You can enter God's Kingdom only through the narrow gate. The highway to hell is broad, and its gate is wide for the many who choose that way.

—MATTHEW 7:13

But many Israelites—those for whom the Kingdom was prepared—will be thrown into outer darkness, where there will be weeping and gnashing of teeth.

—MATTHEW 8:12

Don't be afraid of those who want to kill your body; they cannot touch your soul. Fear only God, who can destroy both soul and body in hell.

—MATTHEW 10:28

The Son of Man will send his angels, and they will remove from his Kingdom everything that causes sin and all who do evil. And the angels will throw them into the fiery furnace, where there will be weeping and gnashing of teeth. Then the righteous will shine like the sun in their Father's Kingdom. Anyone with ears to hear should listen and understand!

—MATTHEW 13:41–43

But what if the servant is evil and thinks, "My master won't be back for a while," and he begins beating the other servants, partying, and getting drunk? The master will return unannounced and unexpected, and he will cut the servant to pieces and assign him a place with the hypocrites. In that place there will be weeping and gnashing of teeth.

—MATTHEW 24:48–51

Then those who were ready went in with him to the marriage feast, and the door was locked. Later, when the other five bridesmaids returned, they stood outside, calling, "Lord! Lord! Open the door for us!" But he called back, "Believe me, I don't know you!"

—MATTHEW 25:10–12

He then began to speak to them in parables: "A man planted a vineyard. He put a wall around it, dug a pit for the winepress and built a watchtower. Then he rented the vineyard to some farmers and went away on a journey. At harvest time he sent a servant to the tenants to collect from them some of the fruit of the vineyard. But they seized him, beat him and sent him away empty-handed. Then he sent another servant to them; they struck this man on the head and treated him shamefully. He sent still another, and that one they killed. He sent many others; some of them they beat, others they killed. He had one left to send, a son, whom he loved. He sent him last of all, saying, 'They will respect my son.' But the tenants said to one another, 'This is the heir. Come, let's kill him, and the inheritance will be ours.' So they took him and killed him, and threw him out of the vineyard. What then will the owner of the vineyard do? He will come and kill those tenants and give the vineyard to others."

—Mark 12:1–9, niv

But I'll tell you whom to fear. Fear God, who has the power to kill you and then throw you into hell. Yes, he's the one to fear.

—Luke 12:5

And you will perish, too, unless you repent of your sins and turn to God.

—Luke 13:3

Then you will say, "But we ate and drank with you, and you taught in our streets." And he will reply, "I tell you, I don't know you or where you come from. Get away from me, all you who do evil." There will be weeping and gnashing of teeth, for you will see Abraham, Isaac, Jacob, and all the prophets in the Kingdom of God, but you will be thrown out.

—Luke 13:26–28

Jesus said, "There was a certain rich man who was splendidly clothed in purple and fine linen and who lived each day in luxury. At his gate lay a poor man named Lazarus who was covered with sores. As Lazarus lay there longing for scraps from the rich man's table, the dogs would come and lick his open sores. Finally, the poor man died and was carried by the angels to be with Abraham. The rich man also died and was buried, and his soul went to the place of the dead. There, in torment, he saw Abraham in the far distance with Lazarus at his side. The rich man shouted, 'Father Abraham, have some pity! Send Lazarus over here to dip the tip of his finger in water and cool my tongue. I am in anguish in these flames.' But Abraham said to him, 'Son, remember that during your lifetime you had everything you wanted, and Lazarus had nothing. So now he is here being comforted, and you are in anguish. And besides, there is a great chasm separating us. No one can cross over to you from here, and no one can cross over to us from there.' Then the rich man said, 'Please, Father Abraham, at least send him to my father's home. For I have five brothers, and I want him to warn them so they don't end up in this place of torment.' But Abraham said, 'Moses and the prophets have warned them. Your brothers can read what they wrote.' The rich man replied, 'No, Father Abraham! But if someone is sent to them from the dead, then they will repent of their sins and turn to God.' But Abraham said, 'If they won't listen to Moses and the prophets, they won't listen even if someone rises from the dead.'"

—Luke 16:19–31

And as for these enemies of mine who didn't want me to be their king—bring them in and execute them right here in front of me.

—Luke 19:27

"Watch out! Don't let your hearts be dulled by carousing and drunkenness, and by the worries of this life. Don't let that day catch you unaware, like a trap. For that day will come upon everyone living on the earth. Keep alert at all times. And pray that you might be strong enough to escape these coming horrors and stand before the Son of Man."

—LUKE 21:34–36

And anyone who believes in God's Son has eternal life. Anyone who doesn't obey the Son will never experience eternal life but remains under God's angry judgment.

—JOHN 3:36

"I tell you the truth, a time is coming and has now come when the dead will hear the voice of the Son of God and those who hear will live. For as the Father has life in himself, so he has granted the Son to have life in himself. And he has given him authority to judge because he is the Son of Man. Do not be amazed at this, for a time is coming when all who are in their graves will hear his voice and come out—those who have done good will rise to live, and those who have done evil will rise to be condemned."

—JOHN 5:25–29, NIV

I have had one message for Jews and Greeks alike— the necessity of repenting from sin and turning to God, and of having faith in our Lord Jesus.

—ACTS 20:21

But because you are stubborn and refuse to turn from your sin, you are storing up terrible punishment for yourself. For a day of anger is coming, when God's righteous judgment will be revealed.

He will judge everyone according to what they have done. He will give eternal life to those who keep on doing good, seeking after the glory and honor and immortality that God offers. But he will pour out his anger and wrath on those who live for themselves, who refuse to obey the truth and instead live lives of wickedness.

—ROMANS 2:5–8

The night is almost gone; the day of salvation will soon be here. So remove your dark deeds like dirty clothes, and put on the shining armor of right living.

—ROMANS 13:12

Instead, clothe yourself with the presence of the Lord Jesus Christ. And don't let yourself think about ways to indulge to your evil desires.

—ROMANS 13:14

Don't you realize that in a race everyone runs, but only one person gets the prize? So run to win! All athletes are disciplined in their training. They do it to win a prize that will fade away, but we do it for an eternal prize. So I run with purpose in every step. I am not just shadowboxing. I discipline my body like an athlete, training it to do what it should. Otherwise, I fear that after preaching to others I myself might be disqualified.

—1 CORINTHIANS 9:24–27

Because we have these promises, dear friends, let us cleanse ourselves from everything that can defile our body or spirit. And let us work toward complete holiness because we fear God.

—2 CORINTHIANS 7:1

When you follow the desires of your sinful nature, the results are very clear: sexual immorality, impurity, lustful pleasures, idolatry, sorcery, hostility, quarreling, jealousy, outbursts of anger, selfish ambition, dissension, division, envy, drunkenness, wild parties, and other sins like these. Let me tell you again, as I have before, that anyone living that sort of life will not inherit the Kingdom of God.

—GALATIANS 5:19–21

He will come with his mighty angels, in flaming fire, bringing judgment on those who don't know God and on those who refuse to obey the Good News of our Lord Jesus. They will be punished with eternal destruction, forever separated from the Lord and from his glorious power.

—2 THESSALONIANS 1:7B–9

Such people claim they know God, but they deny Him by the way they live. They are detestable, disobedient, worthless for doing anything good.

—TITUS 1:16

As for you, Titus, promote the kind of living that reflects wholesome teaching. Teach the older men to exercise self-control, to be worthy of respect, and to live wisely. They must have sound faith and be filled with love and patience. Similarly, teach the older women to live in a way that honors God. They must not slander others or be heavy drinkers. Instead, they should teach others what is good. These older women must train the younger women to love their husbands and their children, to live wisely and be pure, to work in their homes, to do good, and to be submissive to beginning of time—to show us his grace through Christ Jesus.

—2 TIMOTHY 1:9

But God's truth stands firm like a foundation stone with this inscription: "The LORD knows those who are his," and "All who belong to the LORD must turn away from evil."

—2 TIMOTHY 2:19

All Scripture is inspired by God and is useful to teach us what is true and to make us realize what is wrong in our lives. It corrects us when we are wrong and teaches us to do what is right. God uses it to prepare and equip his people to do every good work.

—2 TIMOTHY 3:16–17

I solemnly urge you in the presence of God and Christ Jesus, who will someday judge the living and the dead when he appears to set up his Kingdom: preach the Word of God. Be prepared, whether the time is favorable or not. Patiently correct, rebuke, and encourage your people with good teaching. For a time is coming when people will no longer listen to sound and wholesome teaching. They will follow their own desires and will look for teachers who will tell them whatever their itching ears want to hear. They will reject the truth and chase after myths.

—2 TIMOTHY 4:1–4

For it is impossible to bring back to repentance those who were once enlightened—those who have experienced the good things of heaven and shared in the Holy Spirit, who have tasted the

their husbands. Then they will not bring
on the Word of God. In the same way, enc
the young men to live wisely. And you y
must be an example to them by doing good
of every kind. Let everything you do refl
integrity and seriousness of your teaching
the truth so that your teaching can't be cri
Then those who oppose us will be asham
have nothing bad to say about us.

—TITU

And we are instructed to turn from godles
and sinful pleasures. We should live in t
world with wisdom, righteousness, and dev
God, while we look forward with hope to tl
derful day when the glory of our great G
Savior, Jesus Christ, will be revealed. He g
life to free us from every kind of sin, to cle
and to make us his very own people, tota
mitted to doing good deeds. You must tea
things and encourage the believers to do th
have the authority to correct them when n
so don't let anyone disregard what you say.

—TITUS

Teach these things, Timothy, and en
everyone to obey them. Some people n
tradict our teaching, but these are the wh
teachings of the Lord Jesus Christ. Thes
ings promote a godly life.

—1 TIMOT

For God saved us and called us to live
life. He did this, not because we des
but because that was his plan from be

goodness of the Word of God and the power of the age to come—and who then turn away from God. It is impossible to bring such people back to repentance; by rejecting the Son of God, they themselves are nailing him to the cross once again and holding him up to public shame.

—HEBREWS 6:4–6

Dear friends, if we deliberately continue sinning after we have received knowledge of the truth, there is no longer any sacrifice that will cover these sins. There is only the terrible expectation of God's judgment and the raging fire that will consume his enemies.

—HEBREWS 10:26–27

No discipline is enjoyable while it is happening—it's painful! But afterward there will be a peaceful harvest of right living for those who are trained in this way.

—HEBREWS 12:11

Work at living a holy life, for those who are not holy will not see the Lord.

—HEBREWS 12:14B

Since we are receiving a Kingdom that is unshakable, let us be thankful and please God by worshiping him with holy fear and awe. For our God is a devouring fire.

—HEBREWS 12:28–29

So think clearly and exercise self-control. Look forward to the gracious salvation that will come to you when Jesus Christ is revealed to the world. So you must live as God's obedient children.

Don't slip back into your old ways of living to satisfy your own desires. You didn't know any better then. But now you must be holy in everything you do, just as God who chose you is holy. For the Scriptures say, "You must be holy because I am holy." And remember that the heavenly Father to whom you pray has no favorites. He will judge or reward you according to what you do. So you must live in reverent fear of him during your time as "foreigners in the land." For you know that God paid a ransom to save you from the empty life you inherited from your ancestors. And the ransom he paid was not mere gold or silver. It was the precious blood of Christ, the sinless, spotless Lamb of God. God chose him as your ransom long before the world began, but he has now revealed him to you in these last days. Through Christ you have come to trust in God. And you have placed your faith and hope in God because he raised Christ from the dead and gave him great glory. You were cleansed from your sins when you obeyed the truth, so now you must show sincere love to each other as brothers and sisters. Love each other deeply with all your heart. For you have been born again, but not to a life that will quickly end. Your new life will last forever because it comes from the eternal, living Word of God. As the Scriptures say, "People are like grass; their beauty is like a flower in the field. The grass withers and the flower fades. But the word of the Lord remains forever." And that word is the Good News that was preached to you.

So get rid of all evil behavior. Be done with all deceit, hypocrisy, jealousy, and all unkind speech. Like newborn babies, you must crave pure spiritual milk so that you will grow into a full experience of salvation. Cry out for this nourishment, now that you have had a taste of the Lord's kindness.

—1 Peter 1:13–2:3

By his divine power, God has given us everything we need for living a godly life. We have received all of this by coming to know him, the one who called us to himself by means of his marvelous glory and excellence. And because of his glory and excellence, he has given us great and precious promises. These are the promises that enable you to share his divine nature and escape the world's corruption caused by human desires. In view of all this, make every effort to respond to God's promises. Supplement your faith with a generous provision of moral excellence, and moral excellence with knowledge, and knowledge with self-control, and self-control with patient endurance, and patient endurance with godliness, and godliness with brotherly affection, and brotherly affection with love for everyone. The more you grow like this, the more productive and useful you will be in your knowledge of our Lord Jesus Christ. But those who fail to develop in this way are short sighted or blind, forgetting that they have been cleansed from their old sins. So, dear brothers and sisters, work hard to prove that you really are among those God has called and chosen. Do these things, and you will never fall away. Then God will give you a grand entrance into the eternal Kingdom of our Lord and Savior Jesus Christ.

—2 Peter 1:3–11

For God did not spare even the angels who sinned. He threw them into hell, in gloomy pits of darkness, where they are being held until the day of judgment. And God did not spare the ancient world—except for Noah and the seven others in his family. Noah warned the world of God's righteous judgment. So God protected Noah when he destroyed the world of ungodly people with a vast flood. Later, God condemned the cities of Sodom and Gomorrah and turned them into heaps of ashes. He made them an example of what will happen to ungodly people. But God also rescued Lot out of Sodom because he was a righteous man who was sick of the shameful immorality of the wicked people around him. Yes, Lot was a righteous man who was tormented in his soul by the wickedness he saw and heard day after day. So you see, the Lord knows how to rescue godly people from their trials, even while keeping the wicked under punishment until the day of final judgment. He is especially hard on those who follow their own twisted sexual desire, and who despise authority. These people are proud and arrogant, daring even to scoff at supernatural beings without so much as trembling. But the angels, who are far greater in power and strength, do not dare to bring from the Lord a charge of blasphemy against those supernatural beings. These false teachers are like unthinking animals, creatures of instinct, born to be caught and destroyed. They scoff at things they do not understand, and like animals, they will be destroyed. Their destruction is their reward for the harm they have done. They love to indulge in evil pleasures in broad daylight. They are a disgrace and a stain among you. They delight in deception even as they eat with you in your fellowship meals. They commit adultery with their eyes, and their desire for sin is never satisfied. They lure unstable people into sin, and they are well trained in greed. They live under God's curse. They have wandered off the right road and followed the footsteps of Balaam son of Beor, who loved to earn money by doing wrong. But Balaam was stopped from his mad course when his donkey rebuked him with a human voice. These people are as useless as dried-up springs or as mist blown away by the wind. They are doomed to blackest darkness. They brag about themselves with empty, foolish boasting. With an appeal to twisted sexual desires, they lure back into sin those who have barely escaped from a lifestyle of deception. They promise freedom, but they themselves are slaves of sin and corruption. For you are a slave to whatever controls you. And when people escape from the wickedness of the world by knowing our Lord and Savior Jesus Christ and then get tangled up and enslaved by sin again, they are worse off than before. It would be better if they had never known the way to righteousness than to know it and then reject the command they were given to live a holy life.

—2 PETER 2:4–21

But you must not forget this one thing, dear friends: A day is like a thousand years to the Lord, and a thousand years is like a day. The Lord isn't really being slow about his promise, as some people think. No, he is being patient for your sake. He does not want anyone to be destroyed, but wants everyone to repent.

—2 PETER 3:8–9

So we are lying if we say we have fellowship with God but go on living in spiritual darkness; we are not practicing the truth. But if we are living in the light, as God is in the light, then we have fellowship with each other, and the blood of Jesus, his Son, cleanses us from all sin. If we claim we have no sin, we are only fooling ourselves and not living in the truth. But if we confess our sins to him, he is faithful and just to forgive us our sins and to cleanse us from all wickedness. If we claim we have not sinned, we are calling God a liar and showing that his word has no place in our hearts.

—1 John 1:6–10

And we can be sure that we know him if we obey his commandments. If someone claims, "I know God," but doesn't obey God's commandments, that person is a liar and is not living in the truth. But those who obey God's word truly show how completely they love him. That is how we know we are living in him. Those who say they live in God should live their lives as Jesus did.

—1 John 2:3–6

Do not love this world nor the things it offers you, for when you love the world, you do not have the love of the Father in you. For the world offers only a craving for physical pleasure, a craving for everything we see, and pride in our achievements and possessions. These are not from the Father, but are from this world. And this world is fading away, along with everything that people crave. But anyone who does what pleases God will live forever.

—1 John 2:15–17

And in my vision, I saw the horses and the riders sitting on them. The riders wore armor that was fiery red and dark blue and yellow. The horses had heads like lions, and fire and smoke and burning sulfur billowed from their mouths. One-third of all the people on earth were killed by these three plagues—by the fire and smoke and burning sulfur that came from the mouths of the horses. Their power was in their mouths and in their tails. For their tails had heads like snakes, with the power to injure people. But the people who did not die in these plagues still refused to repent of their evil deeds and turn to God. They continued to worship demons and idols made of gold, silver, bronze, stone, and wood—idols that can neither see nor hear nor walk! And they did not repent of their murders or their witchcraft or their sexual immorality or their thefts.

—REVELATION 9:17–21

Then the fourth angel poured out his bowl on the sun, causing it to scorch everyone with its fire. Everyone was burned by this blast of heat, and they cursed the name of God, who had control over all these plagues. They did not repent of their sins and turn to God and give him glory.

—REVELATION 16:8–9

Then the fifth angel poured out his bowl on the throne of the beast, and his kingdom was plunged into darkness. His subjects ground their teeth in anguish, and they cursed the God of heaven for their pains and sores. But they did not repent of their evil deeds and turn to God.

—REVELATION 16:10–11

Look, I will come as unexpectedly as a thief! Blessed are all who are watching for me, who keep their clothing ready so they will not have to walk around naked and ashamed.

—REVELATION 16:15

Then I heard another voice calling from heaven, "Come away from her, my people. Do not take part in her sins, or you will be punished with her."

—REVELATION 18:4

I saw no temple in the city, for the Lord God Almighty and the Lamb are its temple. And the city has no need of sun or moon, for the glory of God illuminates the city, and the Lamb is its light.... Nothing evil will be allowed to enter, nor anyone who practices shameful idolatry and dishonesty—but only those whose names are written in the Lamb's Book of Life.

—REVELATION 21:22–23, 27

"Look, I am coming soon, bringing my reward with me to repay all people according to their deeds. I am the Alpha and the Omega, the First and the Last, the Beginning and the End." Blessed are those who wash their robes. They will be permitted to enter through the gates of the city and eat the fruit from the tree of life. Outside the city are the dogs— the sorcerers, the sexually immoral, the murderers, the idol worshipers, and all who love to live a lie.

—REVELATION 22:12–15

And if anyone removes any of the words from this book of prophecy, God will remove that person's share in the tree of life and in the holy city that are described in this book.

—REVELATION 22:19

ADDITIONAL READING

Mary K. Baxter, *A Divine Revelation of Hell*
A Divine Revelation of Heaven
A Divine Revelation of The Spirit Realm
A Divine Revelation of Deliverance
A Divine Revelation of Angels
A Divine Revelation of Healing
A Divine Revelation of Prayer

Captain Dale Black, *Flight to Heaven*

Todd Burpo, *Heaven is for Real*

Brian Jones, *Hell Is Real (But I Hate to Admit It)*

Kevin and Alex Malarkey, *The Boy Who Came Back from Heaven*

Don Piper, *90 Minutes in Heaven*

Dennis and Nolene Prince, *Nine Days in Heaven*

Bill Wiese, *23 Minutes in Hell*

All books available online from www.amazon.co.uk or www.wesleyowen.com

NOTES

CHAPTER 1

1. Oswald Chambers, *My Utmost for His Highest*, ed. James Reimann (Grand Rapids, MI: Discovery House, 1992), March 2 entry.
2. Ibid., December 7 entry.

CHAPTER 2

1. Chambers, November 21 entry.

CHAPTER 3

1. Chambers, November 2 entry.

CHAPTER 4

1. Kenneth Barker, *NIV Study Bible* (Grand Rapids, MI: Zondervan, 1995), 1886.

CHAPTER 7

1. Jerry Bridges, *Respectable Sins* (Colorado Springs, CO: NavPress, 2007), 179–180.

APPENDIX A

1. Chambers, December 19 entry.
2. Ibid., December 20 entry.